Thomas Erskine, Richard Baxter, John Gambold, Sam Rutherford

Remarks on the Internal Evidence for the Truth of Revealed Religion

Thomas Erskine, Richard Baxter, John Gambold, Sam Rutherford
Remarks on the Internal Evidence for the Truth of Revealed Religion
ISBN/EAN: 9783743423459
Manufactured in Europe, USA, Canada, Australia, Japa
Cover: Foto ©Lupo / pixelio.de

Manufactured and distributed by brebook publishing software (www.brebook.com)

Thomas Erskine, Richard Baxter, John Gambold, Sam Rutherford

Remarks on the Internal Evidence for the Truth of Revealed Religion

REMARKS

ON THE

INTERNAL EVIDENCE

FOR THE TRUTH OF

𝕽𝖊𝖛𝖊𝖆𝖑𝖊𝖉 𝕽𝖊𝖑𝖎𝖌𝖎𝖔𝖓.

By THOMAS ERSKINE, Esq.

ADVOCATE.

TENTH EDITION.

EDINBURGH:
DAVID DOUGLAS.
1878.

CONTENTS.

REMARKS ON THE INTERNAL EVIDENCE FOR THE TRUTH OF REVEALED RELIGION :—

	PAGE
INTRODUCTORY CHAPTER,	1
SECTION I.	31
SECTION II.	48
SECTION III.	58
SECTION IV.	76
SECTION V.	159
SECTION VI.	178

INTRODUCTORY ESSAYS :—

I. TO GAMBOLD'S WORKS,	209
II. TO BAXTER'S SAINTS' REST,	239
III. TO SAMUEL RUTHERFORD'S LETTERS,	282

INTRODUCTORY CHAPTER.

THERE is a principle in our nature which makes us dissatisfied with unexplained and unconnected facts; which leads us to theorise all the particulars of our knowledge, or to form in our minds some system of causes sufficient to explain or produce the effects which we see; and which teaches us to believe or disbelieve in the truth of any system which may be presented to us, just as it appears adequate or inadequate to afford that explanation of which we are in pursuit. We have an intuitive perception that the appearances of Nature are connected by the relation of cause and effect; and we have also an instinctive desire to classify and arrange the seemingly confused mass of facts with which we are surrounded, according to this distinguishing relationship. From these principles have proceeded all the theories which were ever formed by man. But these principles alone can never make a true theory: they teach us to theorise; but experience is necessary in order to theorise justly. We must be acquainted with the ordinary operation of causes before we can combine them into a theory which will satisfy the mind. But when we are convinced of the real existence of a cause in Nature, and when we find that a class of physical facts is explained by the supposition of this cause, and tallies exactly with its ordinary operation, we resist both reason and instinct when we resist the conviction that this class of facts does result from this cause. On this process of reasoning is grounded our conviction, that the various phenomena of the heavenly bodies are results from the principle or law of gravitation. That great master of theories, Adam Smith, has given a most appropriate and beautiful illustration of this process in his *History of Astronomy*. He has there shown how the speculative system was always accommodated to the phenomena which had been observed;

and how, on each new discovery in point of fact, a corresponding change necessarily took place in the form of the system.

There is another process of reasoning, differing somewhat from that which has been described, yet closely allied to it, by which, instead of ascending from effects to a cause, we descend from a cause to effects. When we are once convinced of the existence of a cause, and are acquainted with its ordinary mode of operation, we are prepared to give a certain degree of credit to a history of other effects attributed to it, provided we can trace the connection between them. As an illustration of this I shall suppose that the steam-engine, and the application of it to the movement of vessels, was known in China in the days of Archimedes; and that a foolish lying traveller had found his way from Sicily to China, and had there seen an exhibition of a steamboat, and had been admitted to examine the mechanical apparatus of it,—and upon his return home, had, amongst many palpable fables, related the true particulars of this exhibition,—what feeling would this relation have probably excited in his audience? The fact itself was a strange one, and different in appearance from anything with which they were acquainted : It was also associated with other stories that seemed to have falsehood stamped on the very face of them. What means, then, had the hearers of distinguishing the true from the false? Some of the rabble might probably give a stupid and wondering kind of credit to the whole; whilst the judicious but unscientific hearers would reject the whole. Now, supposing that the relation had come to the ears of Archimedes, and that he had sent for the man, and interrogated him ; and, from his unorderly and unscientific, but accurate specification of boilers, and cylinders, and pipes, and furnaces, and wheels, had drawn out the mechanical theory of the steamboat,—he might have told his friends, "The traveller may be a liar; but this is a truth. I have a stronger evidence for it than his testimony, or the testimony of any man: it is a truth in the nature of things. The effect which the man has described is the legitimate and certain result of the apparatus which he has described. If he has fabricated this account, he must be a great philosopher. At all events, his narration is founded on an unquestionable general truth." Had the traveller committed an error in his specification, that defect would have operated as an obstacle to the conviction of Archimedes; because, where the facts which are testified constitute the parts of a system, they must, in order to produce conviction, be viewed in their relation to one another, and in their combined bearing on the general result. Unless they are thus viewed, they are not seen as they really exist, —they do not hold their proper ground. A single detached pipe or boiler or valve could not produce the effects of the steam-engine; and a man who knows no more about it than that it contains such a detached part, may very well laugh at the effects related of the whole machine; but, in truth, the fault lies in his own ignorance of the subject.

But these two processes of reasoning which have been described are not exclusively applied to physical causes and effects. We reason precisely in the same way with regard to men and their actions. When the history of a man's life is presented to us, we naturally theorise upon it; and, from a comparison of the different facts contained in it, we arrive at a conviction that he was actuated by ambition, avarice, benevolence, or some other principle. We know that these principles exist, and we know also their ordinary mode of operation. When, therefore, we see the operation, we refer it to the cause which best explains it. In this manner we arrange the characters with which we are acquainted under certain classes; and we anticipate the conduct of our friends when they come to be placed in certain circumstances. And when we are at a distance from any of them, and receive an account of their conduct upon some particular occasion, we give our unhesitating belief at once, if the account coincides with that abstract view which we have taken of their characters; but if it varies very considerably from or is directly opposed to that view, we refuse our immediate belief, and wait for further evidence. Thus, if we hear that a friend, in whose integrity we have perfect confidence, has committed a dishonest action, we place our former knowledge of our friend in opposition to the testimony of our informer, and we anxiously look for an explanation. Before our minds are easy on the subject, we must either discover some circumstance in the action which may bring it under the general principle which we have formed with regard to his character, or else we must form to ourselves some new general principle which will explain it.

We reason in the same way of the intelligence of actions as we do of their morality. When we see an object obtained by means of a plan evidently adapted for its accomplishment, we refer the formation of the plan to design. We reason in this case also from the cause to the effect; and we conclude, that a strong intelligence, when combined with a desire after a particular object, will form and execute some plan adapted to the accomplishment of that particular object. An ambitious man of talents will, we are sure, fix his desires on some particular situation of eminence, and will form some scheme fitted for its attainment. If an intimate and judicious friend of Julius Cæsar had retired to some distant corner of the world, before the commencement of the political career of that wonderful man, and had there received an accurate history of every circumstance of his conduct, how would he have received it? He would certainly have believed it; and not merely because he knew that Cæsar was ambitious, but also because he could discern that every step of his progress, as recorded in the history, was adapted with admirable intelligence to accomplish the object of his ambition. His belief of the history, therefore, would rest on two considerations,—first, that the object attributed by it to Cæsar corresponded with the general principle under which he had classed the moral character of Cæsar; and, secondly, that there was evident, through the course of the history, a perfect adaptation of means to an end. He would have believed just on the same principle that compelled Archimedes to believe the history of the steam-boat.

In all these processes of reasoning we have examples of conviction, upon an evidence which is, most strictly speaking, internal,—an evidence altogether independent of our confidence in the veracity of the narrator of the facts.

Surely, then, in a system which purports to be a revelation from heaven, and to contain a history of God's dealings with men, and to develop truths with regard to the moral government of the universe, the knowledge and belief of which will lead to happiness here and hereafter, we may expect to find (if its pretensions are well founded) an evidence for its truth which shall be independent of all external testimony. But what are the precise principles on which the internal evidence for or against a divine revelation of religion must rest? We cannot have any internal evidence on a subject which is in all its parts and bearings and relations entirely new to us; because, in truth, the internal evidence depends solely on our knowledge that certain causes are followed by certain effects: therefore, if a new train of causes and effects, perfectly different from anything which we have before known, be presented to us, all our notions of probability, all our anticipations of results, and all our references to causes, by which we are accustomed to judge of theories and histories, become utterly useless. In the hypothetical case of Archimedes deciding on the story of the steam-boat, the judgment which he may be supposed to have given was grounded on his belief that similar causes would produce similar effects, and on his experience that the causes which the traveller specified were actually followed in nature by the effects which he specified. The philosopher had never seen this *particular combination of causes;* but he knew each distinct cause with its distinct train of consequents; and thus he anticipated the general result of the combination.

So also the credit attached to the narrative of Cæsar's exploits, by his distant friend, was grounded on the conviction that ambition would lead Cæsar to aim at empire, and on the knowledge that this object could not be attained except by that course which Cæsar pursued. Although the circumstances were new, he could almost have predicted, from analogy, that, whether the design proved finally successful or not, Cæsar would certainly form the design, and construct some such plan for its accomplishment.

Our acquaintance, then, with certain causes as necessarily connected with certain effects, and our intuitive conviction that this same connection will always subsist between these causes and effects, form the basis of all our just anticipations for the future, and of all our notions of probability and internal evidence, with regard to the systems or histories, both physical and moral, which may be presented to us.

If, then, the subject-matter of Divine revelation be entirely new to us, we cannot possibly have any ground on which we may rest our judgment as to its probability. But is this the case with that system of religion which is called Christianity? Is the object which it has in view an entirely new object? Is the moral mechanism which it employs for the accomplishment of that object different in kind from that moral mechanism which we ourselves set to work every day upon our fellow-creatures whose conduct we wish to influence in some particular direction, or from that by which we feel ourselves to be led in the ordinary course of providence? Is the character of the Great Being to whose inspiration this system is ascribed, and whose actions are recorded by it, entirely unknown to us, except through the medium of this revelation? Far from it. Like Archimedes in the case which I have supposed, we have never before seen this *particular combination* of causes brought to bear on this particular combination of results; but we are acquainted with each particular cause, and we can trace its distinct train of consequents; and thus we can understand the relation between the whole of the combined causes and the whole of the combined results.

The first faint outline of Christianity presents to us a view of God operating on the characters of men through a manifestation of his own character, in order that, by leading them to participate, in some measure, of his moral likeness, they may also in some measure participate of his happiness. Every man who believes in the existence of a Supreme Moral Governor, and has considered the relations in which this belief places him, must have formed to himself some scheme of religion analogous to that which I have described. The indications of the Divine character in nature, and providence, and conscience, were surely given to direct and instruct us in our relations to God and his creatures. The indications of his kindness have a tendency to attract our gratitude, and the indications of his disapprobation to check and alarm us. We infer that his own character truly embodies all those qualities which he approves, and is perfectly free from all which he condemns. The man who adopts this scheme of natural religion, which, though deficient in point of practical influence over the human mind, as shall be afterwards explained, is yet true,—and who has learned from experience to refer actions to their moral causes,—is in possession of all the elementary principles which qualify him to judge of the internal evidence of Christianity. He can judge of Christianity as the rude ship-carpenter of a barbarous age could judge of a British ship of the line, or as the scientific anatomist of the eye could judge of a telescope which he had never seen before.

He who holds this scheme of natural religion will believe in its truth (and, I conceive, justly), because it urges him to what is good, deters him from what is evil, and coincides generally with all that he feels and observes; and this very belief which he holds on these grounds will naturally lead him to believe in the truth of another scheme which tends directly to the same moral object, but much more specifically and powerfully, and coincides much more minutely with his feelings and observations.

The perfect moral tendency of its doctrines is a ground on which the Bible often rests its plea of authenticity and importance. What-

ever principle of belief tends to promote real moral perfection possesses in some degree the quality of truth. By moral perfection I mean the perception of what is right, followed by the love of it and the doing of it. This quality, therefore, necessarily implies a true view of the relations in which we stand to all the beings with whom we are connected. In this sense, Pope's famous line is perfectly just,—
"His [faith] can't be wrong, whose life is in the right." But it is evident that a man may be a very useful member of this world's society without ever thinking of the true relation in which he stands to the beings about him. Prudence, honourable feelings, and instinctive good-nature may insure to any man, in ordinary times, an excellent reputation. But the scene of our present contemplation lies in the spiritual universe of God, and the character that we speak of must be adapted to that society. We cannot but believe that true moral perfection contains the elements of happiness in that higher state; and therefore we cannot but believe that that view of our moral relations, and of the beings to whom we are so related, which leads to this moral perfection,

must be the true view. But if the attainment of this character be the important object, why lay so much stress upon any particular view? The reason is obvious. We cannot, according to the constitution of our nature, induce upon our minds any particular state of moral feeling without an adequate cause. We cannot feel anger, or love, or hatred, or fear, by simply endeavouring so to feel. In order to have the feeling, we must have some object present to our minds which will naturally excite the feeling. Therefore, as moral perfection consists of a combination of moral feelings, leading to correspondent action, it can only have place in a mind which is under the impression, or has a present view of those objects which naturally produce that combination of feelings.

The object of this Dissertation is to analyse the component parts of the Christian scheme of doctrine, with reference to its bearings both on the character of God and on the character of man; and to demonstrate that its facts not only present an expressive exhibition of all the moral qualities which can be conceived to reside in the Divine mind, but also contain all those objects which have a natural tendency to excite and suggest in the human mind that combination of moral feelings which has been termed moral perfection. We shall thus arrive at a conclusion with regard to the facts of revelation, analogous to that at which Archimedes arrived with regard to the narrative of the traveller,—viz., a conviction that they contain a general truth in relation to the characters both of God and of man; and that therefore the Apostles must either have witnessed them, as they assert, or they must have been the most marvellous philosophers that the world ever saw. Their system is true in the nature of things, even were they proved to be impostors.

When God, through his prophet Jeremiah, refutes the pretensions of the false teachers of that day, he says,—" If they had stood in my counsel, and had caused my people to hear my words, then they should have turned them from their evil way, and from the evil of their doings." This moral tendency of its doctrines, then, is the evidence which the book itself appeals to for the proof of its authenticity; and surely it is no more than justice that this evidence should be candidly examined. This is an evidence, also, on which the apostle Paul frequently rests the whole weight of the gospel.

According to this theory of the mode in which a rational judgment of the truth and excellence of a religion may be formed, it is not enough to show, in proof of its authenticity, that the facts which it affirms concerning the dealings of God with his creatures do exhibit his moral perfections in the highest degree; it must also be shown that these facts, when present to the mind of man, do naturally, according to the constitution of his being, tend to excite and suggest that combination of feelings which constitutes his moral perfection. But when we read a history which authoritatively claims to be an exhibition of the character of God in his dealings with men,— if we find in it that which fills and overflows our most dilated conceptions of moral worth and loveliness in the Supreme Being, and at the same time feel that it is triumphant in every appeal that it makes to our consciences, in its statements of the obliquity and corruption of our own hearts,—and if our reason further discovers a system of powerful moral stimulants, embodied in the facts of this history, which necessarily tend to produce in the mind a resemblance to that high character which is there portrayed,—if we discern that the spirit of this history gives peace to the conscience by the very exhibition which quickens its sensibility—that it dispels the terrors of guilt by the very fact which associates sin with the full loathing of the heart—that it combines in one wondrous and consistent whole our most fearful forebodings, and our most splendid anticipations for futurity—that it inspires a pure and elevated and joyful hope for eternity, by those very declarations which attach a deeper and more interesting obligation to the discharge of the minutest part of human duty,—if we see that the object of all its tendencies is the perfection of moral happiness, and that these tendencies are naturally connected with the belief of its narration, —if we see all this in the gospel, we may then say that our own eyes have seen its truth, and that we need no other testimony: we may then well believe that God has been pleased, in pity to our wretchedness, and in condescension to our feebleness, to clothe the eternal laws which regulate his spiritual government, in such a form as may be palpable to our conceptions, and adapted to the urgency of our necessities.

This theory of internal evidence, though founded on analogy, is yet essentially different in almost all respects from that view of the subject which Bishop Butler has given in his most valuable and philosophical work on the analogy of natural and revealed religion. His design was to answer objections against revealed religion, arising out of the difficulties connected with many of its doctrines, by showing that precisely the same difficulties occur in natural religion and in the ordinary course of providence. This argument converts even the difficulties of revelation into evidences of its genuineness; because it employs them to establish the identity of the Author of Revelation and the Author of Nature. My object is quite different. I mean to show that there is an intelligible and necessary connection between the doctrinal facts of revelation and the character of God (as deduced from natural religion), in the same way as there is an intelligible and necessary connection between the character of a man and his most characteristic actions; and further, that the belief of these doctrinal facts has an intelligible and necessary tendency to produce the Christian character, in the same way that the belief of danger has an intelligible and necessary tendency to produce fear.

Perhaps it may appear to some minds that, although all this should be admitted, little or no weight has been added to the evidence for the truth of revelation. These persons have been in the habit of thinking that the miraculous inspiration of the Scriptures is the sole point of importance: whereas the inspiration, when demonstrated, is no more than an evidence for the truth of that system which is communicated through this channel. If the Christian system be true, it would have been so although it had never been miraculously revealed to men. This principle, at least, is completely recognised with regard to the moral precepts. The duties of justice and benevolence are acknowledged to be realities altogether independent of the enforcements of any inspired revelation. The character of God is just as immutable, and as independent of any inspired revelation, as these duties; and so also are the acts of government proceeding from this character. We cannot have stronger evidence for any truth whatever than that which we have for the reality of moral obligations. Upon this basis has been reared the system of natural religion as far as relates to the moral character of God, by simply clothing the Supreme Being with all the moral excellencies of human nature in an infinite degree. A system of religion which is opposed to these moral obligations is opposed also to right reason. This sense of moral obligation then, which is the standard to which reason instructs man to adjust his system of natural religion, continues to be the test by which he ought to try all pretensions to Divine revelation. If the actions ascribed to God by any system of religion present a view of the Divine character which is at variance with the idea of moral perfection, we have no reason to believe that these are really the actions of God. But if, on the contrary, they have a strong and distinct tendency to elevate and dilate our notions of goodness, and are in perfect harmony with these notions, we have reason to believe that they may be the actions of God; because they are intimately connected with those moral convictions which form the first principles of all our reasonings on this subject. This, then, is the first reasonable test of the truth of a religion—that it should coincide with the *moral* constitution of the human mind. But, secondly, we know, that, independently of all moral reasoning or consideration, our minds, by their *natural* constitution, are liable to receive certain impressions from certain objects when present to them. Thus, without any exercise of the moral judgment, they are liable to the impressions of love and hatred, and fear and hope when certain corresponding objects are presented to them. And it is evident that the moral character is determined by the habitual direction which is given to these affections. Now if the actions attributed to God by any system of religion be really such objects as, when present to the mind, do not stir the affections at all, that religion cannot influence the character, and is therefore utterly useless. If they be such as do indeed rouse the affections, but at the same time give them a wrong direction, that religion is worse than useless— it is pernicious. But if they can be shown to be such as have a necessary tendency to excite these natural emotions on the behalf of goodness, and to draw the current of our affections and wills into this moral channel, we are entitled to draw another argument, from this circumstance, in favour of the truth of that religion; because we may presume that God would suit his communications to the capacities and instincts of his creatures. The second test, then, of the truth of a religion is—that it should coincide with the *physical* constitution of the human mind. But, further, there is much moral evil and much misery in the world. There are many bad passions in the mind; and there is a series of events continually going forward, which tend to excite a great variety of feelings. Now, a religion has one of the characters of truth when it is accommodated to all these circumstances,— when it offers pardon without lowering the standard of moral duty; when its principles convert the varied events into opportunities of growing in conformity to God, and of acquiring the character of happiness; and when it tempers the elevation of prosperity, and the depression of adversity. The third test, then, of the truth of a religion is,—that it should coincide with the *circumstances* in which man is found in this world. It may be said that a religion in which these three conditions meet, rests upon the most indisputable axioms of the science of human nature. All these conditions can be proved to meet in the religion of the Bible; and the wide divergence from them which is so palpable in all other religious systems, philosophical as well as popular, which have come to our knowledge, is a very strong argument for the divine inspiration of the Bible, especially when the artless simplicity of its manner, and the circumstances of the country in which it was written, are taken into consideration.

It may be proper to remark, that the acts attributed to the Divine government are usually termed "doctrines," to distinguish them from the moral precepts of a religion.

When I make use of the terms "manifestation" and "exhibition," which I shall have frequent occasion to do in the course of the following observations, I am very far from meaning anything like a mere semblance of action without the substance. In fact, nothing can be a true manifestation of the Divine character, which is not, at the same time, a direct and necessary result of the Divine principles, and a true narration of the Divine conduct. But these terms suit best with the leading idea which I wish to explain,—viz., that the facts of revelation are developments of the moral principles of the Deity, and carry an influential address to the feelings of man. The whole of their importance, indeed, hinges upon their being a reality; and it is the truth of this reality which is demonstrated by their holy consistency with the character of their Author, and their sanctifying applicability to the hearts of his creatures. I may observe also, that, in the illustrations which are introduced, I have aimed rather at a broad and general resemblance than at a minute coincidence in all particulars, which is perhaps not attainable in any comparison between earthly things and heavenly.

I. As it is a matter of the very highest importance in the study of religion, to be fully satisfied that there is a real connection between happiness and the knowledge and love of God,

I have commenced these remarks by explaining the nature of this connection. I have here endeavoured to show that the object of a true religion must be to present to the minds of men such a view of the character of their great Governor as may not only enable them to comprehend the principles of his government, but may also attract their affections into a conformity with them.

II. I have made some observations on the mode in which natural religion exhibits the Divine character, and in which it appeals to the human understanding and feelings. And here I have remarked the great advantage which a general principle of morality possesses in its appeals to minds constituted like ours, when it comes forth to us in the shape of an intelligible and palpable action, beyond what it possesses in its abstract form.

III. I have attempted to show that Christianity possesses this advantage in the highest degree; that its facts are nothing more than the abstract principles of natural religion, embodied in perspicuity and efficiency;[1] and that these facts not only give a lively representation of the perfect character of God, but also contain in themselves the strength of the most irresistible moral arguments that one man could address to another on any human interests.

IV. I have endeavoured to analyse some of

[1] This last proposition, which appeared as it now stands, in former editions of this work, has been subjected to considerable censure, and not without justice as it has been understood. Had I meant by this, that the facts of Christianity could have been anticipated by any one who was acquainted with the principles of natural religion—or that no new information was communicated by the gospel, I should have been opposing the claim, and giving up the importance of revelation. Man never could have discovered the plan of salvation, but after it is revealed, he can perceive its agreement with those principles which had been previously acknowledged. That God must always act in consistency with both justice and mercy, the natural religionist believes; but how these attributes can be brought into harmonious contact in the restoration of the guilty, he knows not. When, however, the doctrine of the cross of Christ is understood by him, he immediately recognises in it the full maturity and development of principles which he had known in their elementary seeds. The information of the gospel is new, but not strange. Two recognised attributes of the Deity are manifested in a new connection, but no new attribute is introduced. I should now prefer that the proposition had been expressed differently, as thus, "That its facts do embody in perspicuity and efficiency the abstract principles of natural religion." I am aware also that there is a considerable vagueness in the term "natural religion;" but there is no other word for it, and metaphysical accuracy is not of much moment here.

the causes of the general indifference to or rejection of real Christianity, and to point out the sources of the multiplied mistakes which are made with regard to its nature. I have here made some observations on the indisposition of the human mind to attend to an argument which opposes any favourite inclination; on the opposition of Christianity to the prevailing current of the human character; and on the bad effects arising from the common practice of deriving our notions of religion rather from the compositions of men than from the Bible. Infidels are not in general acquainted, through the Bible itself, with the system of revelation; and therefore they are inaccessible to that evidence for it which arises out of the discovery that its doctrinal facts all tally exactly with the character which its precepts inculcate. I have here also illustrated this coincidence between the doctrines and the precepts of the Bible in several particulars. If the Christian character is the character of true and immortal happiness, the system must be true which necessarily leads to that character.

V. I have endeavoured to show the need that men have for some system of spiritual renovation; and I have inferred from the preceding argument, that no such system could be really efficient, unless it resembled Christianity in its structure and mode of enforcement.

VI. I have shown the connection between the external and internal evidence for revelation.

ON THE INTERNAL EVIDENCE FOR THE TRUTH OF REVEALED RELIGION.

SECTION I.

WHEN it is said that happiness is necessarily and exclusively connected with a resemblance to the Divine character, it is evident that the word "happiness" must be understood in a restricted sense. It cannot be denied that many vicious men enjoy much gratification through life; nor can it even be denied that this gratification is derived in a great measure from their very vices. This fact is, no doubt, very perplexing, as every question must be which is connected with the origin of evil: but still, it is no more perplexing than the origin of evil, or than the hypothesis that our present life is a state of trial and discipline. Temptation to evil evidently implies a sense of gratification proceeding from evil; and evil could not have existed without this sense of gratification connected with it. So, also, this life could not be a state of trial and discipline in good, unless there were some inducement or temptation to evil,—that is, unless there were some sense of gratification attending evil. It probably does not lie within the compass of human faculties to give a completely satisfactory answer to these questions; whilst yet it may be rationally maintained, that if there is a propriety in this life being a state of discipline, there must also be a propriety in sin being connected with a sense of gratification. But then, may not this vicious gratification be extended through eternity, as well as through a year or an hour? I cannot see any direct impossibility in this supposition, on natural principles; and yet I feel that the assertion of it sounds very much like the contradiction of an intuitive truth.

There is a great difference between the happiness enjoyed with the approbation of conscience, and that which is felt without it or against it. When the conscience is very sensitive, the gratification arising from vice cannot be very great: the natural process, therefore, by which such gratification is obtained or heightened, is by lulling or deadening the conscience. This is accomplished by habitually turning the attention from the distinction of good and evil, and directing it to the circumstances which constitute vicious gratification.

The testimony of conscience is that verdict which every man returns for or against himself upon the question, whether his moral character has kept pace with his moral judgment. This verdict will therefore be, in relation to absolute moral truth, correct or incorrect, in proportion to the degree of illumination possessed by the moral judgment; and the feeling of remorse will be more or less painful according to the inequality which subsists between the judgment and the character. When a man, therefore, by dint of perseverance, has brought his judgment down to the level of his character, and has trained his reason to call evil good and good evil, he has gained a victory over conscience, and expelled remorse. If he could maintain this advantage through his whole existence his conduct would admit of a most rational justification. But then, his peace is built solely on the darkness of his moral judgment; and therefore, all that is necessary in order to make him miserable, and to stir up a civil war within his breast, would be to throw such a strong and indubious light on the perfect character of goodness, as might extort from him an acknowledgment of its excellency, and force him to contrast with it his own past history and present condition. Whilst his mental eye is held in fascination by this glorious vision, he cannot but feel the anguish of remorse; he cannot but feel that he is at fearful strife with some mighty and mysterious being, whose power has compelled even his own heart to execute vengeance on him; nor can he hide from himself the loathsomeness and pollution of that spiritual pestilence, which has poisoned every organ of his moral constitution. He can hope to escape from this wretchedness only by withdrawing his gaze from the appalling brightness; and, in this world, such an attempt can generally be made with success. But suppose him to be placed in such circumstances that there should be no retreat—no diversity of objects which might divert or divide his attention—

and that, wherever he turned, he was met and fairly confronted by this threatening Spirit of Goodness,—it is impossible that he could have any respite from misery, except in a respite from existence. If this should be the state of things in the next world, we may form some conception of the union there between vice and misery.

Whilst we stand at a distance from a furnace, the effect of the heat on our bodies gives us little uneasiness ; but as we approach it, the natural opposition manifests itself, and the pain is increased by every step that we advance. The complicated system of this world's business and events forms, as it were, a veil before our eyes, and interposes a kind of moral distance between us and our God, through which the radiance of his character shines but indistinctly, so that we can withhold our attention from it if we will: The opposition which exists between his perfect holiness and our corrupt propensities does not force itself upon us at every step: His views and purposes may run contrary to ours ; but as they do not often meet us in the form of a direct and personal encounter, we contrive to ward off the conviction that we are at hostility with the Lord of the Universe, and think that we may enjoy ourselves in the intervals of these much-dreaded visitations, without feeling the necessity of bringing our habits into a perfect conformity with his. But when death removes this veil, by dissolving our connection with this world and its works, we may be brought into a closer and more perceptible contact with Him who is of purer eyes than to behold iniquity. In that spiritual world we may suppose that each event, even the minutest part of the whole system of government, will bear such an unequivocal stamp of the Divine character, that an intelligent being, of opposite views and feelings, will at every moment feel itself galled and thwarted and borne down by the direct and overwhelming encounter of this all-pervading and almighty mind. And here it should be remembered, that the Divine government does not, like human authority, skim the surface, nor content itself with an unresisting exterior and professions of submission; but comes close to the thoughts, and carries its summons to the affections and the will, and penetrates to those recesses of the soul, where, whilst we are in this world, we often take a pride and a pleasure in fostering the unyielding sentiments of hatred and contempt, even towards that superiority of force which has subdued and fettered and silenced us.

The man who believes in revelation will, of course, receive this view as the truth of God; and even the unbeliever in revelation, if he admits the existence of an almighty Being of a perfect moral character, and if he see no unlikelihood in the supposition that the mixture of good and evil, and the process of moral discipline connected with it, are to cease with this stage of our being, even he cannot but feel that there is a strong probability in favour of such an anticipation.

We see, then, how vicious men may be happy to a certain degree in this world, and yet be miserable in the next, without supposing any very great alteration in the general system of God's government, and without taking into account anything like positive infliction as the cause of their misery. And it may be observed, that this view gives to vice a form and an extent and a power very different from what is generally ascribed to it amongst men. We are here conversant chiefly about externals; and therefore the name of vice is more commonly applied to external conduct than to internal character. But in the world of spirits it is not so. *There*, a dissonance in principle and object from the Father of spirits constitutes vice, and is identified with unhappiness; so that a man who has here passed a useful and dignified life, upon principles different from those of the Divine character, must, when under the direct action of that character, feel a want of adjustment and an opposition which cannot but mar or exclude happiness. Thus, also, the effects of pride, of vanity, or of selfishness, when combined with prudence, may often be most beneficial in the world; and yet, if these principles are in opposition to God's character, they must disqualify the minds in which they reign, for participating in the joys of heaven. The joys of heaven are described in Scripture to consist in a resemblance to God, or in a cheerful and sympathising submission to his will; and as man naturally follows the impulse of his own propensities, without reference to the will of God, it is evident that a radical change of principle is necessary, in order to capacitate him for that happiness.

It was to produce this necessary and salutary change that the gospel was sent from heaven. It bears upon it the character of God. It is not, therefore, to be wondered at, that those whose principles are opposed to that character should also be opposed to the gospel. Christianity thus anticipates the discoveries of death: it removes the veil which hides God from our sight; it brings the system of the spiritual world to act upon our consciences; it presents us with a specimen of God's higher and interior government; it gives us a nearer view of his character in its true proportions, and thus marks out to us the points in which we differ from him; it condemns with his authority; it smiles and invites with his uncompromising purity. The man who dislikes all this will reject Christianity, and replace the veil, and endeavour to forget the awful secrets which it conceals; and may perhaps be only at last roused from his delusion, by finding himself face to face before the God whose warnings he had neglected, and whose offers of friendship he had disregarded,—offers which, had they been accepted, would have brought his will into concord with that sovereign will which rules the universe, and fitted him to take a joyful and sympathising interest in every part of the Divine administration.

Of the attractive and overcoming loveliness of the character of God, as revealed in his word, and of the invitations which he makes to sinners, I shall speak afterwards; but in the meantime I would draw the attention of the reader to the serious consideration of the fact, that a dissonance in principle from the Ruler of the Universe cannot but be connected with some degree of unhappiness. Although I believe that few minds will feel much difficulty in acquiescing in some measure in the truth of this remark, and although there is no intricacy in the reasoning connected with it, yet, as distinct conceptions on this subject are of prime importance in all views of religion, I shall illustrate it by an analogy drawn from the more palpable and better understood affairs of this material world with which we are surrounded. We may find striking examples to this purpose in a period of English history which was distinguished above all others for the remarkable contrasts which it exhibited in public sentiment and principle amongst the different classes of the nation, and is therefore peculiarly fitted for elucidating the effects produced on happiness by an opposition in principle between the ruling power and a part of its subjects.

It is easy to imagine the stern and composed satisfaction with which a thorough partisan of Cromwell would contemplate the rigid and formal solemnity which overspread the Government and the people of England during the Protectorship. But whence did this satisfaction arise? Certainly from that concord which subsisted between his own habits and those of the ruling power. His views and inclinations coincided at all points with those of the Government; and therefore every measure of administration was a source of gratification to him, because it was in fact an expression of his own will. He was thus in a state of political happiness; and had there been no higher government than the Commonwealth, through the universe or through eternity, he must have been perfectly and permanently happy. Now, let us carry forward this same individual to the days of Charles the Second, and place him in the near neighbourhood of that gay and dissolute Court. We can in this situation suppose him moving about with a double measure of gloom in his countenance, and with a heart embittered by the general mirth, and irritated by the continual encounter of character and opinions and habits directly opposed to his own. He retires to a distance from the seat of Government, and endeavours to hide himself from these painful conflicts in the bosom of his family. There the arrangements are all conducted according to his own principles and his own taste; and he enjoys a tolerable state of happiness, though liable to occasional interruptions from public news, from whispers that he is to be apprehended on suspicion of treason, from the intrusion of Government officers, and from a want of thorough sympathy on political subjects even perhaps in the members of his own domestic circle. All at once his quiet is destroyed by an order from court to leave his seclusion, and reside in the metropolis, that he may be more immediately under the eye of Government. Here again he is brought face to face with all that he hates and despises. His aversion is increased by a sense of his inability to resist; and he learns even to cherish the feeling and habit of misery as the only testimony that his soul is unsubdued. He is politically miserable. I have given this sketch as an illustration of those natural laws which make our happiness dependent on our sympathy with a power which overrules us; and also as an example of the form and the precariousness of that process by which we can in some circumstances contract our horizon, as it were, and shut out from our view those things which give us pain, and withdraw ourselves from the encounter of those principles which are in opposition to our own. In the field of this world there are many divisions and subdivisions, separated by strong barriers from each other, and acknowledging different authorities, or the same authority perhaps in different degrees. These are so many shelters to which men may betake themselves, when pursued by the justice or injustice of their fellow-creatures. But whilst we continue within the scope of one authority, although we may find a temporary asylum against its enmity in a narrower circle or more private society, we are continually liable to be confronted by it, and dragged from our hiding-place; and must, therefore, from the nature of things, be in some measure dependent on it for our happiness.

Whenever the material world and its concerns are made use of to illustrate the concerns of the mind and of the invisible world, it is of great importance to preserve in lively recollection the essential difference which separates the two subjects. The one embraces outward actions exclusively; whilst the prominent feature in the other is the principle from which the actions spring. Thus, in the example which has just been given, we can easily suppose that Cromwell's followers were actuated by a great variety of motives, and that the solemnity of the Commonwealth might captivate different minds on very different principles. Some pious people might have liked it, from having associated it in their minds with true religion; some from the fanatical idea that this outward form would atone for more secret sins; some from its mixture with republican sturdiness; and some, from a hatred of Popery or of the Stuart family. Now, these principles are all very different in their nature, although their external results might in some particulars resemble each other; and therefore the happiness of the citizens did not proceed from an actual *sympathy of principle* with the Government, but *from a coincidence in the effects* of their principles. And if the Government had had cognisance and control of the mind as well as the body, then those alone could have been happy, or could have been considered as good citizens, who liked that solemn system of things precisely on the same principles with the Government; and the collision of opposite principle would in this case have been as violent as the collision of external conduct actually was. In morals an action does not mean an effect simply, but a principle carried into exercise; and therefore, in a government of minds, any effect produced by pride, for instance, however beneficial to the public, would get the name of a proud action, and would be condemned by a judge who disapproved of pride. Man cannot see into the heart, and therefore he is obliged to conjecture or guess at principles by their effects; but yet his judgment is always determined by the nature of the principle to which he ascribes the effects. Supposing, then, that we were under such a supernaturally gifted government, and that this government was so strong that the idea of resisting or escaping it involved an absurdity,—it would evidently become a matter of the very highest importance to make ourselves accurately acquainted with its principles, and to accommodate our own to them; because, till this were accomplished, we could never enjoy tranquillity, but must continually suffer the uneasiness of being reluctantly borne down by the current of a will more powerful than our own. This object, however, would be attended by considerable difficulty. In the first place, it could not be very easy to discover the precise principles of the administration: Almost any single act might proceed from a great variety of principles; and it would therefore require a long observation and induction of facts, in order to arrive at a satisfactory conclusion. And, in the second place, after we had discovered those principles, we might chance to find that they were in direct opposition to our own.

In these circumstances, it would be most desirable that the Government should, for the information of the people, embody in one interesting train of action the whole of the principles of its administration; so that an unequivocal and distinct idea of these principles might be conveyed, by the narrative, to any one who would carefully consider its purport. After Government had done this, it would evidently be the interest and the duty of all the subjects to dwell much upon the history thus communicated to them, in order that they might in this way familiarise their minds to the principles developed in it, and teach their own thoughts to run in the same channel, and interest their affections and feelings in it as much as possible. The people would engage in this with greater or less earnestness, according to the strength or weakness of the conviction which each one had as to the reality of the connection which subsisted between happiness and the accomplishment of this object, and also in proportion to their persuasion that this history was a true representation of the character of the Government. Approbation and affection could alone constitute the necessary adjustment. Fear might urge to the prosecution of the object, but the complete harmony of the will is the result of a more generous principle. If we suppose, further, that this complete harmony of sentiment is one of the great objects of Government, then a coincidence on the part of the subjects, unless connected with a distinct intention to coincide, could not contain in itself the elements of a complete harmony, because it did not embrace this great object of the Government.

SECTION II.

I HAVE made these remarks for the purpose of illustrating the object of the Christian revelation, and of explaining the necessity of believing its announcement, in order to the full accomplishment of that object in each individual case. The object of Christianity is to bring the character of man into harmony with that of God. To this end it is evidently necessary that a just idea of the Divine character should be formed. The works of creation, the arrangements of providence, and the testimony of conscience, are, if thoroughly weighed, sufficient to give this idea: but men are in general so much occupied by the works, that they forget their great Author; and their characters are so opposed to his, that they turn away their eyes from the contemplation of that purity which condemns them. And even in the most favourable cases, the moral efficiency of the idea presented by these natural lights is much hindered and weakened by the abstractness and vagueness of its form.

When we look into creation or providence for the indication of God's character, we are struck with the mixture of appearances which present themselves. We see on one side, life, health, happiness; and on the other, death, disease, pain, misery. The first class furnishes us with arguments for the goodness of God; but what are we to make of the opposite facts? The theory on this subject which is attended with fewest difficulties is founded on two suppositions,—first, That moral good is necessary to permanent happiness; and second, That misery is the result of moral evil, and was appointed by the Author of Nature as its check and punishment. This theory throws some light on the character both of God and of man. It represents God not merely as generally solicitous for the happiness of men, but as solicitous to lead them to happiness through the medium of a certain moral character, which is the object of his exclusive approbation; and it represents man as very sinful, by holding forth the mass of natural evil in the world as a sort of measure of his moral deficiency; and suggests that the disease must be indeed virulent when so strong a medicine is necessary. The fact, however, that the greatest natural evil does not always fall where moral evil is most conspicuous, whilst it gives rise to the idea of a future state, does nevertheless obscure, in some degree, our ideas of the divine character. Our notion of the goodness of God, according to natural religion, does not then arise so much from the knowledge of any one distinct unequivocal manifestation of that quality, as from a general comparison of many facts, which, when combined, lead to this conclusion. This remark applies also to our notion of the divine holiness, or God's exclusive approbation of one particular character; though not to the same extent,—because conscience comes much more directly to the point here than reason does in the other case. The excitements and motives, arising out of such a comparison as has been described, cannot be nearly so vivid or influential as those which spring from the belief of a simple and unequivocal fact which recurs to us without effort, and unfolds its instruction without obscurity, and which holds out to us an unvarying standard, by which we may at all times judge of the thoughts and intentions of God in his dealings with men. Natural theology, therefore, becomes almost necessarily rather a subject of metaphysical speculation than a system of practical principles. It marks the distinctions of right and wrong; but it does not efficiently attach our love to what is right, nor our abhorrence to what is wrong. We may frequently observe real serious devotedness, even amongst the professors of the most absurd superstitions; but it would be difficult to find a devoted natural religionist. The reason is, that these superstitions, though they have no relation to the true character of God, have yet some applicability to the natural constitution of man. Natural religion possesses the former qualification in much greater perfection than the latter. Under an impression of guilt, a man who has no other religious knowledge than that which unassisted reason affords must feel much perplexity and embarrassment.

He believes that God is gracious; but the wounds which he feels in his own conscience, and the misery which he sees around him, demonstrate also that God is of a most uncompromising purity. He knows not what to think; and he is tempted either to despair, or to turn his thoughts away entirely from so alarming a subject. All these conditions of mind—despair, thoughtlessness, and perplexity—are equally adverse to the moral health of the soul, and are equally opposed to that zealous and cheerful obedience which springs from gratitude for mercy, and esteem for holy and generous worth. In such circumstances, the mind would naturally, in self-defence, contrive to lower its standard of moral duty down to the level of its own performances; or would settle into a gloomy hostility to a lawgiver who requires more from it than it is disposed to render. It is in this form of weakness and perversion that we generally see natural religion; and we need not wonder at this melancholy phenomenon, when we consider that its principles consist in abstract conclusions of the intellect, which make no powerful appeal to the heart.

A single definite and intelligible action gives a vividness and power to the idea of that moral character which it exhibits, beyond what could be conveyed by a multitude of abstract descriptions. Thus the abstract ideas of patriotism and integrity make but an uninteresting appearance, when contrasted with the high spectacle of heroic worth which was exhibited in the conduct of Regulus, when, in the senate of his country, he raised his solitary voice against those humbling propositions of Carthage, which, if acquiesced in, would have restored him to liberty, and which, for that single reason, had almost gained an acquiescence; and then, unsubdued alike by the frantic entreaties of his family, the weeping solicitations of the admiring citizens, and the appalling terrors of his threatened fate, he returned to Africa, rather than violate his duty to Rome and the sacredness of truth.

In the same way, the abstract views of the Divine character, drawn from the observation of nature, are in general rather visions of the intellect than efficient moral principles in the heart and conduct; and, however true they may be, are uninteresting and unexciting when compared with the vivid exhibition of them in a history of definite and intelligible action.

To assist our weakness, therefore, and to accommodate his instructions to the principles of our nature, God has been pleased to present to us a most interesting series of actions, in which his moral character, as far as we are concerned, is fully and perspicuously embodied. In this narration the most condescending and affecting and entreating kindness is so wonderfully combined with the most spotless holiness, and the natural appeals which emanate from every part of it to our esteem, our gratitude, our shame, and our interest, are so urgent and constraining, that he who carries about with him the conviction of the truth and reality of this history possesses in it a principle of mighty efficiency, which must subdue and harmonise his mind to the will of that Great Being whose character is there depicted.

The delineation of the character of an overruling authority, whatever that character may be, makes a strong appeal to the subjects on the score of their interest: It calls upon them, as they value their happiness, to bring their own views into conformity with it. The appeal becomes more forcible and effectual, if the character which they are thus called on to contemplate be such a one as would naturally excite esteem and affection in an uninterested observer. But the weight of the appeal is infinitely increased when this powerful and amiable Being is represented to them in the attitude of a benefactor, exerting this power and putting forth this character on their own peculiar behalf.

It is thus that the character of God is represented in the New Testament; and it is on these grounds that we are called on to love, to obey, and to imitate him. If God's character be in fact such as is there described, then those who reject the history in which this character is developed shut themselves out from the opportunity of familiarising their minds to the Divine government, and of bringing their affections and their views to harmonise with it.

There is a divine beauty and wisdom in the form in which God has chosen to communicate the knowledge of his character, which, when duly considered, can scarcely fail of exciting gratitude and admiration. The object of the gospel is to bring man into harmony with God; the subject of its operations, therefore, is the human heart in all its various conditions. It addresses the learned and the unlearned, the savage and the civilised, the decent and the profligate; and to all it speaks precisely the same language. What then is this universal language? It cannot be the language of metaphysical discussion, or what is called abstract moral reasoning; for this could be intelligible to few, and it could influence the characters of fewer. The principles which it addresses ought evidently to be such as are in a great measure independent of the extremes of cultivation and barbarism; and, in point of fact, they are so. They are indeed the very principles which Mr. Hume designates to be "a species of natural instincts, which no reasoning or process of the thought or understanding is able either to produce or to prevent."[1] Its argument consists in a relation of facts: if these are really believed, the effect on the character necessarily follows. It presents a history of wondrous love, in order to excite gratitude; of

[1] *Inquiry into Human Understanding*, sec. v. pt. 1.

high and holy worth, to attract veneration and esteem: it presents a view of danger, to produce alarm; of refuge, to confer peace and joy; and of eternal glory, to animate hope.

SECTION III.

THE reasonableness of a religion seems to me to consist in there being a direct and natural connection between a believing of the doctrines which it inculcates, and a being formed by these to the character which it recommends. If the belief of the doctrines has no tendency to train a disciple in a more exact and more willing discharge of its moral obligations, there is evidently a very strong probability against the truth of that religion. In other words, the doctrines ought to tally with the precepts, and to contain in their very substance some urgent motives for the performance of them; because, if they are not of this description, they are of no use. What is the history of another world to me, unless it have some intelligible relation to my duties or happiness? If we apply this standard to the various religions which different nations have framed for themselves, we shall find very little matter for approbation, and a great deal for pity and astonishment. The very states which have chiefly excelled in arts and literature and civil government have failed here most lamentably. Their moral precepts might be very good; but then these precepts had as much connection with the history of astronomy as with the doctrines of their religion. Which of the adventures of Jupiter, or Brama or Osiris could be urged as a powerful motive to excite a high moral feeling, or to produce a high moral action? The force of the moral precepts was rather lessened than increased by the facts of their mythology. In the religion of Mahomet there are many excellent precepts; but it contains no illustration of the character of God which has any particular tendency beyond or even equal to that of natural religion to enforce these precepts. Indeed, one of the most important doctrines which he taught,—viz., a future life beyond the grave,—from the shape which he gave to it, tended to counteract his moral precepts. He described it as a state of indulgence in sensual gratifications which never cloyed the appetite; and yet he preached temperance and self-denial. It is evident that any self-restraint which is produced by the belief of this doctrine must be merely external; for the real principle of temperance could not be cherished by the hope of indulgence at a future period. The philosophical systems of theology are no less liable to the charge of absurdity than the popular superstitions. No one can read Cicero's work on the Nature of the Gods, without acknowledging the justice of the Apostle's sentence upon that class of reasoners,—" professing themselves to be wise, they became fools."

As the principles and feelings of our nature which are addressed in religion are precisely the same with those which are continually exercised in the affairs of this world, we may expect to find a resemblance between the doctrines of a true religion and the means and arguments by which a virtuous man acquires an influence over the characters and conduct of his fellow-creatures. When a man desires another to do anything, that is the precept; when he enforces it by any mode of persuasion, that is the doctrine. When the Athenians were at war with the Heraclidæ, it was declared by the Oracle that the nation whose king died first should be victorious in the contest. As soon as this was known, Codrus disguised himself, went over to the camp of the enemy, and exposed himself there to a quarrel with a soldier, who killed him without knowing who he was. The Athenians sent to demand the body of their king; which so alarmed the Heraclidæ, from the recollection of the Oracle, that they fled in disorder. Now, let us suppose that Codrus wished to inculcate the principle of patriotism in his countrymen. If he had merely issued a proclamation commanding every citizen to prefer the interest of his country to his own life, he would have been giving them a moral precept, but without a corresponding doctrine. If he had joined to this proclamation the promise of honour and wealth as the rewards of obedience, he would have been adding a very powerful doctrine, yet nevertheless such a doctrine as must have led much more directly to patriotic conduct than to patriotic feeling and principle. Vanity and avarice, without patriotism, might have gained those rewards. But if he wished to excite or to cherish the principle of patriotism in the hearts of his people, he chose the most eloquent and prevailing argument, when he sacrificed his life for them, and thus attracted their admiration and gratitude to that spirit which animated his breast, and their love to that country of which he was at once the representative and the ransom.

It is indeed a striking and yet an undeniable fact, that we are comparatively little affected by abstract truths in morality. The cry of a child will produce a greater movement, in almost any mind, than twenty pages of unanswerable reasoning. An instinctive acquaintance with this fact guides us in our dealings with our fellow-creatures; and He who formed the heart of man has attested his revealed word by showing his acquaintance with the channel through which persuasion and instruction might be most effectually communicated. It may therefore be useful to illustrate at greater length the analogy which exists between the persuasions of the gospel and those which might be fixed on as the most powerful arguments capable of being addressed to any human feelings on the subject of human interests.

Let us, then, present to ourselves a company of men travelling along the sea-shore. One of them, better acquainted with the ground than the rest, warns them of quicksands, and points out to them a landmark which indicated the position of a dangerous pass. They, however, see no great reason for apprehension; they are anxious to get forward, and cannot resolve upon making a considerable circuit in order to avoid what appears to them an imaginary evil; they reject his counsel, and proceed onward. In these circumstances, what argument ought he to use? What mode of persuasion can we imagine fitted to fasten on their minds a strong conviction of the reality of their danger, and the disinterested benevolence of their adviser? His words have been ineffectual; he must try some other method; he must act. And he does so; for, seeing no other way of prevailing on them, he desires them to wait only a single moment, till they see the truth of his warning confirmed by his fate. He goes before them; he puts his foot on the seemingly firm sand, and sinks to death. This eloquence is irresistible: he was the most active and vigorous among them; if any one could have extricated himself from the difficulty it was he; they are persuaded; they make the necessary circuit, bitterly accusing themselves of the death of their generous companion; and during their progress, as often as these landmarks occur, his nobleness and their own danger rise to their minds, and secure their safety. Rashness is now not perilous merely —it is ungrateful; it is making void the death of their deliverer.

To walk without God in the world is to walk in sin; and sin is the way of danger. Men had been told this by their own consciences, and they had even partially and occasionally believed it; but still they walked on. Common arguments had failed; the manifestations of the Divine character in creation and providence, and the testimony of conscience, had been in a great measure disregarded. It thus seemed necessary that a stronger appeal should be made to their understanding and their feelings. The danger of sin must be more strikingly and unequivocally demonstrated; and the alarm excited by this demonstration must be connected with a more kindly and generous principle, which may bind their affections to that

God from whom they have wandered. But how is this to be done? What more prevailing appeal can be made? Must the Almighty warner demonstrate the evil of sin by undergoing its effects? Must he prove the danger of sin by exhibiting himself as a sufferer under its consequences? Must he who knew no sin suffer as a sinner, that he might persuade men that sin is indeed an evil?—It was even so. God became man, and dwelt amongst us. He himself encountered the terrors of guilt, and bore its punishment; and called on his careless creatures to consider and understand the evil of sin, by contemplating even its undeserved effects on a being of perfect purity, who was over all, God blessed for ever. Could they hope to sustain that weight which had crushed the Son of God? Could they rush into that guilt and that danger against which he had so pathetically warned them? Could they refuse their hearts and their obedience to him who had proved himself so worthy of their confidence?—especially when we consider that this great Benefactor is ever present, and sees the acceptance which this history of his compassion meets with in every breast, rejoicing in those whose spirits are purified by it, and still holding out the warning of his example to the most regardless.

Ancient history tells us of a certain king who made a law against adultery, in which it was enacted that the offender should be punished by the loss of both eyes. The very first offender was his own son. The case was most distressing; for the king was an affectionate father, as well as a just magistrate. After much deliberation and inward struggle, he finally commanded one of his own eyes to be pulled out and one of his son's. It is easier to conceive than to describe what must have been the feelings of the son in these most affecting circumstances. His offence would appear to him in a new light; it would appear to him not simply as connected with painful consequences to himself, but as the cause of a father's sufferings, and as an injury to a father's love. If the king had passed over the law altogether, in his son's favour, he would have exhibited no regard for justice, and he would have given a very inferior proof of affection. We measure affection by the sacrifice which it is prepared to make, and by the resistance which it overcomes. If the sacrifice had been made, and the resistance overcome secretly in the heart of the king, there could have been but little evidence of the real existence either of principle or of affection; and the son might perhaps have had reason to think that his pardon was as much the effect of his father's disregard of the law as of his affection to him: and at any rate, even if he had given the fullest credit to the abstract justice and kindness which were combined in his acquittal, it is impossible that this theoretical character of his father could have wrought on his heart any impression half so energetic, or interesting, or overwhelming, as that which must have been produced by the simple and unequivocal and practical exhibition of worth which has been recorded. If we suppose that the happiness of the young man's life depended on the eradication of this criminal propensity, it is not easy to imagine how the king could more wisely or more effectually have promoted this benevolent object. The action was not simply a correct representation of the king's character,—it also contained in itself an appeal most correctly adapted to the feelings of the criminal. It justified the king in the exercise of clemency; it tranquillised the son's mind, as being a pledge of the reality and sincerity of his father's gracious purposes towards him; and it identified the object of his esteem with the object of his gratitude. Mere gratitude, unattracted by an object of moral worth, could never have stamped an impression of moral worth on his character; which was his father's ultimate design. We might suppose the existence of this same character without its producing such an action; we might suppose a conflict of contending feelings to be carried on in the mind without evidencing, in the conduct flowing from it, the full vehemence of the conflict, or defining the adjustment of the contending feelings; but we cannot suppose any mode of conduct so admirably fitted to impress the stamp of the father's character on the mind of the son, or to associate the love of right and the abhorrence of wrong with the most powerful instincts of the heart. The old man not only wished to act in perfect consistency with his own views of duty, but also to produce a salutary effect on the mind of his son; and it is the full and effectual union of these two objects which forms the most beautiful and striking part of this remarkable history.

There is a singular resemblance between this moral exhibition and the communication which God has been pleased to make of himself in the gospel. We cannot but love and admire the character of this excellent prince, although we ourselves have no direct interest in it; and shall we refuse our love and admiration to the King and Father of the human race, who, with a kindness and condescension unutterable, has, in calling his wandering children to return to duty and to happiness, presented to each of us a like aspect of tenderness and purity, and made use of an argument which makes the most direct and irresistible appeal to the most familiar, and at the same time the most powerful principles in the heart of man?

In the gospel God is represented in the combined character of a gracious parent and a just judge. His guilty children are arraigned before him and condemned: they have not only forfeited all claim to his favour, by the breach of that fundamental law which binds all intelligent creatures to love and resemble their Creator; but they have also by the same means contracted the disease of sin, and lost that mental health which can alone capacitate for spiritual enjoyment. Thus, the consistency of their Judge, and their own diseased condition, seemed equally to cover their futurity with a pall of the deepest mourning. This disease constituted their punishment. Pardon, whilst this disease remained, was a mere name: mercy, therefore, if at all communicated, must be communicated in such a way as to heal this disease—in such a way as to associate sin with the abhorrence of the heart, and duty with the love of the heart. The exhibition of the Divine character in this dispensation of mercy must not only be consistent with its own excellence, but also suited to make an impression on the reason and the feelings of the guilty. And it is so. The Judge himself bore the punishment of transgression, whilst he published an amnesty to the guilty, and thus asserted the authority and importance and worth of the law, by that very act which beamed forth love unspeakable, and displayed a compassion which knew no obstacle but the unwillingness of the criminals to accept it. The Eternal Word became flesh; and exhibited, in sufferings and in death, that combination of holiness and mercy, which, believed, must excite love, and if loved, must produce resemblance.

A pardon without a sacrifice could have made but a weak and obscure appeal to the understanding or the heart. It could not have demonstrated the evil of sin; it could not have demonstrated the graciousness of God; and, therefore, it could not have led man either to hate sin or to love God. If the punishment as well as the criminality of sin consists in an opposition to the character of God, the fullest pardon must be perfectly useless, whilst this opposition remains in the heart; and the substantial usefulness of the pardon will depend upon its being connected with such circumstances as may have a natural and powerful tendency to remove this opposition, and create a resemblance. The pardon of the gospel is connected with such circumstances; for the sacrifice of Christ has associated sin with the blood of a benefactor, as well as with our own personal sufferings,—and obedience with the dying entreaty of a friend breathing out a tortured life for us, as well as with our own unending glory in his blessed society. This act, like that in the preceding illustration, justifies God as a lawgiver in dispensing mercy to the guilty; it gives a pledge of the sincerity and reality of that mercy; and, by associating principle with mercy, it identifies the object of gratitude with the object of esteem, in the heart of the sinner. It may also here be observed, that the resurrection and ascension of Christ, as the representative of our race, not only demonstrate the Divine complacency in the work of the Saviour, but exhibit to us also the indissoluble connection which subsists between immortal glory and an entire unreserved acquiescence in the will of God; and thus the Christian hope is not directed to an undefined ease and enjoyment in heaven, but to a defined and intelligible happiness springing from the more perfect exercise of those very principles of love to God and man which formed the character of their Master, and still constitute his joy.

The distinction of persons in the Divine nature we cannot comprehend; but we can easily comprehend the high and engaging morality of that character of God which is developed in the history of the New Testament. God gave his equal and well-beloved Son to suffer in the stead of an apostate world; and through this exhibition of awful justice he publishes the fullest and freest pardon. He thus teaches us, that it forms no part of his scheme of mercy to dissolve the eternal connection between sin and misery. No; this connection stands sure; and one of the chief objects of Divine revelation is to convince men of this truth. And Justice does the work of mercy when it alarms us to a sense of danger, and stimulates us to flee from a continually increasing woe. But the cross of Christ does not merely show the danger of sin; it demonstrates an unwearied compassion,—a love unutterable, which extends its invitations and entreaties of reconciliation as wide as the ravages of sin, in order that by such an instance of self-sacrificing solicitude on the part of God for their welfare, men might be allured to the love of Him who had so loved them; and that their grateful admiration having for its object the full perfections of the Divine character, might gradually carry them forward to an entire resemblance of it.

Most men will have no hesitation to admit the general proposition that the moral character of God supposes the union of justice and mercy in an infinite degree. Now, the gospel history simply gives an individuality and a life to this general idea, in the same way that the old king's conduct toward his son gave an individuality and a life to the general idea of paternal affection in union with a regard for the laws. Most men will also admit that the conduct of this good prince was suited not only to give a distinct view of his own principles, but also to stamp the character of these principles on the heart of his son. But the same causes operate in fitting the conduct of God, as declared in the gospel, for stamping the character of its principles on the hearts of those who believe it. The old king was sensible that the abstract idea of his justice and affection would have had but very little influence on his son's character; and, therefore, it was the part of a wise and benevolent man to embody this abstract idea in a palpable action, which might make an intelligible and powerful appeal to his understanding and his heart. The abstract idea of God's character has still less influence on our minds; because the invisible infinity of his essence adds incalculably to the natural vagueness and inefficiency of such impressions. It was therefore the part of a wise and benevolent Being to embody his attributes in a train of palpable and intelligible action, which might carry a distinct and influential appeal to our capacities and feelings. If the ultimate object of God's dealings with men had been to pardon their sins, this might have been done without giving them any information on the subject until they stood before the judgment-seat. But if his gracious object was as the Bible represents it, to make men partakers of his own happiness, by communicating to them his own moral likeness, it was necessary that such an exhibition of his moral character should be made to them as might convey to their understandings a distinct idea of it, and might address to their feelings of gratitude and esteem and interest such appropriate excitements and persuasives as might lead to a full resemblance of it.

SECTION IV.

But many who admit the abstract character of God feel, notwithstanding, a disposition to reject the gospel history; although its whole tenor is in perfect conformity with the general idea to which they have professed their consent. This is natural, though unreasonable. It is probable that the old king's son was very much astonished when he learned the final determination as to the mode of executing the law in his case; yet if he had been asked before, what his opinion of his father's character was, it is likely that he would have answered with confidence that he knew him to be a just prince and an affectionate father. Why, then, was he astonished? Did not the fact agree with his previous judgment? The only explanation is, that he did not comprehend the full meaning of his own expressions; and when he saw the general idea which he had formed of his father's character embodied in an action, he did not recognise it to be in fact the same thing. Many of those who reason on the character of God fall into a similar mistake: they admit his absolute moral perfections; but when the abstract idea which they have formed of Him takes life before their eyes, and assumes the body of an action, they start from it as if it were an utter stranger. And why? The only reason which can be given is, that the abstract idea which they talk about is so vague and indeterminate, as to make no distinct impression on their minds.

If a man really admitted, in truth and in intelligence, that abstract idea of God which he admits in words, he would find his reason compelled to believe a fact which is only an exemplification of that idea, nay the existence of which seems in some degree indispensable to the consistency of that idea. The admission of this abstract idea, and the rejection of the corresponding fact, are as inconsistent as to be convinced of the thorough liberality of a friend's character, and at the same time to reject as absurd and fanciful the history of a liberal action said to have been performed by him when the occasion seemed actually to require it.

There is another quality belonging to abstract ideas, arising from the vagueness of the impressions made by them, which recommends them to many minds; and that is, their inoffensiveness. A corrupt politician, for instance, can speculate on and applaud the abstract idea of integrity; but when this abstract idea takes the form of a man and a course of action, it ceases to be that harmless and welcome visitor it used to be, and draws on itself the decided enmity of its former apparent friend. The fact is, that the man never really loved the abstract idea of integrity, else he must have loved every exemplification of it. We have thus an unequivocal test of a man's principles. Bring the eloquent eulogist of magnanimity into a situation where he may be tried,—bring him in difficult circumstances into contact with a person of real magnanimity, —and we shall see whether it was the thing or the name which he loved.

In the same way, many men will admit the abstract idea of a God of infinite holiness and goodness; and will even take delight in exercising their reason or their taste in speculating on the subject of his being and attributes; yet these same persons will shrink with dislike and alarm from the living energy which this abstract idea assumes in the Bible. It is there no longer a harmless generality: it is a living Being, asserting one spiritual character and one class of principles in harmony with his own, disapproving and condemning every other, and casting the weight of omnipotence into his scale, to prove the vanity of all resistance. Those who feel oppressed by the vigilance and strictness of this ever-present witness, without being convinced of the importance of his friendship, are glad to retreat and to shroud themselves under the vagueness of an abstract idea. But in truth they do not believe nor love this abstract idea of God, else they would also believe and love the living character which corresponds to it. The real conviction of the truth of the abstract idea would necessarily contain in it the conviction of the corresponding fact.

These remarks may serve to illustrate the grounds on which a charge of moral guilt is brought by the Scriptures against unbelief.

If a man cannot refuse his assent and approbation to an abstract principle in morals, why does he reject it when it loses its abstractness, and comes in a form of power and efficiency? The principle continues the same; it has only assumed a more active attitude. In truth, he now rejects it because it is active, and because it strenuously opposes many of his favourite inclinations. He does not wish to be guided by what he knows to be right, but by what he feels to be agreeable. "He does not wish to retain God in his knowledge." He does not wish, at any risk, or with any sacrifice, to do the will of God; and *therefore* "he doth not know of the doctrine whether it be of God." Such an ignorance as this is criminal; because it arises from a wilful stifling of conviction, and an aversion to admitted truths.

It thus appears, that, by the help of abstract ideas and general terms, a man may appear to have made great progress in morals, whilst in fact he has learned nothing. Things operate on our minds exactly according to our apprehension of them, and not according to their own intrinsic value. Our apprehension of abstract truths in morality is so vague, that they hardly operate on our characters at all. Does it not, then, approach almost to a demonstration, that if God really intended to improve the happiness and characters of men, by instructing them in the excellence of his own character, he would communicate this instruction, not in the form of abstract propositions and general terms, which are, by the construction of the human mind, incapable of producing any real and lasting effect upon us, but by that way which coincides with our faculties of apprehension,—that is, by the way of living and palpable actions, which may add the weight and distinctness of their own substance to those truths which they are intended to develop? That men stand in need of such an improvement is certain; that a gracious Being should intend it is surely not improbable; and if he had such an intention, that some such scheme as Christianity should have been adopted seems necessary to its success.

At first sight, it may seem strange that a system evidently flowing from so much goodness, tending to so much happiness, and constructed with so much wisdom, should in general be either rejected, or admitted with an inattentive and therefore useless assent. But there are circumstances in the case which abundantly account for this. The great author of Christianity anticipated this rejection, and forewarned his disciples of it. His knowledge of the heart of man made him well acquainted with many causes which would operate against the reception of his doctrine. When Agis attempted to regenerate the diseased government of Sparta, he stirred up and armed against himself all the abuses and corruptions of the state. It would have been strange if this had not happened; and it would also be strange, if a doctrine which tends to regenerate human nature, and to eradicate the deep-seated and yet favourite diseases of the heart, should not arm against itself all those moral evils which it threatens to destroy.

A man finds no difficulty in giving his acquiescence to any proposition which does not carry along with it an obligation on him to something which he dislikes. The great bulk of the population of this country, for instance, acquiesce in the Copernican system of astronomy, although they may possess little or no knowledge of the mathematical or physical truths on which this system is reared. But let us make the supposition for a moment, that an acquiescence in this theory somehow or other involved in it a moral obligation on every believer in it to walk round the world, we cannot doubt but that the party of Ptolemy, or some other less imperious philosopher, would, in these circumstances, very soon carry almost every voice.

The religion of Jesus Christ involves in it a great variety of obligations; and it was indeed principally for the purpose of elucidating and enforcing these obligations that God was pleased to make it known to mankind. And many of these obligations are so distasteful to the natural selfishness or indolence of our hearts, that we feel unwilling to embrace a conviction which involves in it so complete a derangement of our plans, and a thwarting of our habitual inclinations. Were the beautiful lineaments of the Christian character to be portrayed in a theory which should disclaim all interferences with the consciences and duties of the world, it would infallibly attract much intellectual and sentimental admiration; and were the high and holy character of God, and its universally-pervading influence, to be painted in glowing colours,—and were that unbounded liberty to be described in which those spirits that areperfectly conformed to His will must expatiate through all the vastness of creation and eternity,—were all this to be couched in the terms of a lofty imagination, without any appeal to the conscience, and without attempting to bring in this splendid vision to haunt our hours of carelessness or of crime,—who can doubt that taste, and fancy, and eloquence would pour in their converted disciples within the engaging circle of such a religion? And yet we find that taste, and fancy, and eloquence, and high intellect, and fine sentiment often reject Christianity : and the reason seems to be, because it is not a science merely, but a practical art, in which every part of knowledge is connected with a corresponding duty. It does not present to us a beautiful picture merely,—it commands us to copy it; it does not merely hold forth to us the image of perfect virtue,—it declares to us also our own guilt, and denounces our condemnation ; it does not merely exhibit to us the sublime idea of a spiritual and universal sovereign,—it also calls upon us, by this very exhibition, under the most awful sanctions of hope and fear, to humble ourselves before Him, and to look to Him as the rightful proprietor of our thoughts and words and actions. There is something in all this very harassing and unpleasing to our nature; and the fact that it is so may account for the real rejection that it generally meets with even amongst its nominal friends, and may also operate as a warning against ascribing too much weight to that contempt or aversion which it sometimes receives from those whose talents, when directed to other objects, we have been accustomed to follow with our admiration and gratitude. The proud man does not like to give up the triumph of superiority; the vain man does not like to give up the real or fancied applause of the circle in which he moves; the careless or worldly or sensual man does not like to have himself continually watched and scrutinised by a witness who never sleeps, and who is of purer eyes than to behold iniquity. Now, as great talents are often to be found in men of such characters, we need not wonder that they employ these talents in defending the foundation on which their chief enjoyment is built, rather than in pursuit of a truth which, they are conscious, would level the whole fabric with the ground. Men do not look very diligently for that which they would be sorry to find.

It is difficult to persuade a careless profligate to live a life of temperate and useful exertion; because it is difficult to obtain from him a candid hearing on the subject. He thinks exclusively of the gratifications which he is called upon to renounce, and never allows his mind to rest calmly on the motives which would induce him to do so. Whilst he apprehends fully and distinctly the pleasures connected with his own habits, he has a very vague idea of the evils resulting from them, or of the advantages of an opposite course. If the latter apprehension were as vivid as the former, the man's character would change. And there are arguments, and those of a mere worldly nature, which have often produced this effect. All that is necessary to accomplish it is a candid attention on his part to the whole truth of the case. There is in his mind, indeed, a natural opposition to the argument;

but there is also in the argument a natural destructiveness of his faults; and if it be vividly apprehended and retained, it will gain the victory, and cast out its enemy. The argument, then, must, in the first place, be a sufficient one in itself; that is to say, it must show, that, in reason, the advantage gained by complying with it exceeds the advantage of rejecting it. And, in the second place, this sufficient argument must be distinctly and fully apprehended. The best argument in the world is of no use, unless it be properly understood, and the motives which it holds forth be vividly apprehended. To a mind that does not distinctly comprehend the subject, a good argument will appear bad, and a bad one may appear good. We account, in this way, for the different success which the same argument meets with when it is addressed to a number of individuals. Some are moved by it—others are not; that is to say, some fully apprehend it—others do not. And this may arise either from their misunderstanding the terms of the argument, or from their unwillingness to admit a principle which interferes with their own inclinations.

Thus it fares often with human arguments; nor do the arguments of God escape a similar fate. We have already seen how the spirituality of the Christian requirements naturally excites an unwillingness to admit its principles. This unwillingness can only be overcome by a full view of its glorious inducements. But, unfortunately, this view is often intercepted and obscured by various causes, and by none more than the usual way in which religion is studied.

Most people in this country, and probably even the majority of the population in Europe, think that they understand Christianity; and yet a very small proportion of them have read the Bible with that degree of ordinary attention which they bestow on the common concerns of life. Their ideas on this subject are derived almost entirely from creeds and church articles, or human compositions of some kind. The evil consequences arising from this are most grievous. To convince ourselves that they are indeed so to a high degree we have only to compare the two methods.

In the Bible we uniformly find the doctrines—even those that are generally considered most abstruse—pressed upon us as demonstrations or evidences of some important moral feature of the Divine mind, and as motives tending to produce in us some corresponding disposition in relation to God or man. This is perfectly reasonable. Our characters cannot but be in some degree affected by what we believe to be the conduct and the will of the Almighty toward ourselves and the rest of our species. The history of this conduct and this will constitutes what are called the Christian doctrines. If, then, the disposition, or character which we are urged to acquire, recommend itself to our reasons and consciences as right and agreeable to the will of God, we cannot but approve that precept as morally true; and if the doctrine by which it is enforced carries in it a distinct and natural tendency to produce this disposition or character, then we feel ourselves compelled to admit that there is at least *a moral truth* in this doctrine. And if we find that the doctrine has not only this purely moral tendency, but that it is also most singularly adapted to assert and acquire a powerful influence over those principles in our nature to which it directs its appeal, then we must also pronounce that there is a natural truth in the doctrine,—or, in other words, that however contradictory it may be to human practice, it has, however, a natural consistency with the regulating principles of the human mind. And further, if the doctrine be not only true in morals and in its natural adaptation to the mind of man, but if the fact which it records coincides also and harmonises with that general idea of the Divine character which reason forms from the suggestions of conscience, and from an observation of the works and ways of God in the external world, then we are bound to acknowledge that this doctrine appears to be true in its relation to God. In the Bible the Christian doctrines are always stated in this connection: they stand as indications of the character of God, and as the exciting motives of a corresponding character in man. Forming thus the connecting link between the character of the Creator and the creature, they possess a majesty which it is impossible to despise, and exhibit a form of consistency and truth which it is difficult to disbelieve. Such is Christianity in the

Bible; but in creeds and church articles it is far otherwise. These tests and summaries originated from the introduction of doctrinal errors and metaphysical speculations into religion: and, in consequence of this, they are not so much intended to be the repositories of truth, as barriers against the encroachment of erroneous opinions. The doctrines contained in them therefore are not stated with any reference to their great object in the Bible,—the regeneration of the human heart, by the knowledge of the Divine character. They appear as detached propositions, indicating no moral cause, and pointing to no moral effect. They do not look to God, on the one hand, as their source; nor to man, on the other, as the object of their moral urgency. They appear like links severed from the chain to which they belonged; and thus they lose all that evidence which arises from their consistency, and all that dignity which is connected with their high design. I do not talk of the propriety or impropriety of having church articles, but the evils which spring from receiving impressions of religion exclusively or chiefly from this source.

I may instance the ordinary statement of the doctrine of the Trinity, as an illustration of what I mean. It seems difficult to conceive that any man should read through the New Testament candidly and attentively without being convinced that this doctrine is essential to and implied in every part of the system: but it is not so difficult to conceive, that although his mind is perfectly satisfied on this point, he may yet, if his religious knowledge is exclusively derived from the Bible, feel a little surprised and staggered, when he for the first time reads the terms in which it is announced in the articles and confessions of all Protestant churches. In these summaries the doctrine in question is stated by itself, divested of all its scriptural accompaniments; and is made to bear simply on the nature of the Divine essence, and the mysterious fact of the existence of Three in One. It is evident that this fact, taken by itself, cannot in the smallest degree tend to develop the Divine character, and therefore cannot make any moral impression on our minds.

In the Bible it assumes quite a different shape; it is there subservient to the manifestation of the moral character of God. The doctrine of God's combined justice and mercy in the redemption of sinners, and of his continued spiritual watchfulness over the progress of truth through the world, and in each particular heart, could not have been communicated without it, so as to have been distinctly and vividly apprehended: but it is never mentioned except in connection with these objects; nor is it ever taught as a separate subject of belief. There is a great and important difference between these two modes of statement. In the first the doctrine stands as an isolated fact of a strange and unintelligible nature, and is apt even to suggest the idea that Christianity holds out a premium for believing improbabilities. In the other it stands indissolubly united with an act of Divine holiness and compassion, which radiates to the heart an appeal of tenderness most intelligible in its nature and object, and most constraining in its influence.

The abstract fact that there is a plurality in the unity of the Godhead really makes no address either to our understandings, or our feelings, or our consciences. But the obscurity of the doctrine, as far as moral purposes are concerned, is dispelled, when it comes in such a form as this,—"God so loved the world, that he gave his only begotten Son, that whosoever believeth in him might not perish, but have everlasting life." Or this,—"But the Comforter, which is the Holy Ghost, whom the Father will send in my name, he shall teach you all things." Our metaphysical ignorance of the Divine essence is not indeed in the slightest degree removed by this mode of stating the subject; but our moral ignorance of the Divine character is enlightened; and that is the thing with which we have to do. We love or hate our fellow-creatures—we are attracted to or repelled from them—in consequence of our acquaintance with their moral characters; and we do not find ourselves barred from the exercise of these feelings, because the anatomical structure of their frames is unknown to us, or because the mysterious link which binds the soul to the body has baffled all investigation. The knowledge communicated by revelation is a moral knowledge, and it has been communicated in order to produce a moral effect upon our characters; and a knowledge of the Divine essence would have as little bearing upon this object, as far as we can see, as a knowledge of the elementary essence of matter.

I shall give one example more of the mode in which the truth of God has been perverted by passing through the hands of men. The doctrine of the atonement through Jesus Christ, which is the corner-stone of Christianity, and to which all the other doctrines of revelation are subservient, has had to encounter the misapprehension of the understanding as well as the pride of the heart. This pride is natural to man, and can only be overcome by the power of the truth; but the misapprehension might be removed by the simple process of reading the Bible with attention; because it has arisen from neglecting the record itself, and taking our information from the discourses or the systems of men who have engrafted the metaphysical subtleties of the schools upon the unperplexed statement of the word of God. In order to understand the facts of revelation, we *must* form a system to ourselves; but if any subtlety, of which the application is unintelligible to common sense, or uninfluential on conduct, enters into our system, we may be sure that it is a wrong one. The common-sense system of a religion consists in two connections,—first, the connection between the doctrines and the character of God which they exhibit; and secondly, the connection between these same doctrines and the character which they are intended to impress on the mind of man. When, therefore, we are considering a religious doctrine, our questions ought to be: first, What view does this doctrine give of the character of God in relation to sinners? and secondly, What influence is the belief of it calculated to exercise on the character of man? Though I state the questions separately, my observations on them cannot properly be kept entirely distinct. The first of these questions leads us to consider the atonement as an act necessarily resulting from and simply developing principles in the Divine mind, altogether independent of its effects on the hearts of those who are interested in it. The second leads us to consider the adaptation of the history of the atonement, when believed, to the moral wants and capacities of the human mind. This last consideration really embraces the former; because it is only by the impressions produced on our minds by any being whatever, that we can judge of the qualities of that being. And the impressions produced by the atonement are referrible to its adaptation to the human mind. There is something very striking and wonderful in this adaptation; and the deeper we search into it, the stronger reasons shall we discover for admiration and gratitude, and the more thoroughly shall we be convinced that it is not a lucky coincidence, nor an adjustment contrived by the precarious and temporising wisdom of this world, but that it is stamped with the uncounterfeited seal of the universal Ruler, and carries on it the traces of that same mighty will which has connected the sun with his planetary train, and fixed the great relations in nature, appointing to each atom its bound that it cannot pass. Yet it must be remembered that this adaptation is only an evidence for the truth of the gospel, but that it does not constitute the gospel. The gospel consists in the proclamation of mercy through the sacrifice of Jesus Christ. This is the only true source of sanctity and peace and hope,—and if, instead of drinking from this fountain, we busy ourselves in tracing the course of the streams that flow from it, and in admiring the beauty and fertility of the country through which they run, we may indeed have a tasteful and sentimental relish for the organisation of Christianity, but it will not be in us a well of water springing up into everlasting life. Before we admit the truth of a doctrine like the atonement it is proper to contemplate it in all its consequences; but after we have admitted it, we ought to give the first place in our thoughts to the doctrine itself, because our minds are usefully operated on, not by the thought of the consequences, but by the contemplation of the doctrine. When an act of kindness has been done to us, our gratitude is excited by contemplating the kindness itself, not by investigating that law in our nature by which gratitude naturally is produced by kindness. It is of great importance to remember this. We do not and cannot become Christians by thinking of the Christian character, nor even by thinking of the adaptation of the Christian doctrines to produce that character, but by having our hearts impressed and imbued by the doctrines themselves. The doctrines are constituent parts of God's character and government, and they are revealed to us that we may be renewed in the spirit of our minds by the knowledge of them.

The doctrine of the atonement is the great subject of revelation. God is represented as delighting in it, as being glorified by it, and as being most fully manifested by it. All the other doctrines radiate from this as their centre. In subservience to it, the distinction in the unity of the Godhead has been revealed. It is described as the everlasting theme of praise and song amongst the blessed who surround the throne of God. It is represented in language suitable to our capacities, as calling forth all the energies of omnipotence. And, indeed, when we come to consider what this great work was, we shall not wonder that even the inspired heralds of salvation faltered in the utterance of it. The human race had fallen off from their allegiance, they had turned away from God, their hearts chose what God abhorred, and despised what God honoured: they were the enemies of God, they had broken his law, which their own consciences acknowledged to be holy, just, and gracious, and had thus most righteously incurred the penalty denounced against sin. Man had thus ruined himself, and the faithfulness of God seemed bound to make this ruin irretrievable.

The design of the atonement was to make mercy towards this offcast race consistent with the honour and the holiness of the Divine government. To accomplish this gracious purpose the Eternal Word, who was God, took on himself the nature of man, and as the elder brother and representative and champion of the guilty family, he solemnly acknowledged the justice of the sentence pronounced against sin, and submitted himself to its full weight of woe, in the stead of his adopted kindred. God's justice found rest here; his law was magnified and made honourable. The human nature of the Saviour gave him a brother's right and interest in the human race, whilst his divine nature made his sacrifice available, and invested the law, under which he had bowed himself, with a glory beyond what could have accrued to it from the penal extinction of a universe. The two books of the Bible in which this subject is most minutely and methodically argued, viz., the Epistles to the Romans and the Hebrews, commence with asserting most emphatically both the perfect divinity and the perfect humanity of Jesus Christ. On this basis the reasoning is founded which demonstrates the universal sufficiency and the suitableness of the death of Christ as an atonement for the sins of men, or as a vindication of the justice of the Divine government in dispensing mercy to the guilty. What a wonderful, and awful, and enlivening subject of contemplation this is! God so loved the world that he gave his only begotten Son, that whosoever believeth on him might not perish, but have everlasting life. And the same God, that he might declare his abhorrence of sin in the very form and substance of his plan of mercy, sent forth this Son to make a propitiation *through his blood.* This is the God with whom we have to do. This is his character, the Just God and yet the Saviour. There is an augustness and a tenderness about this act, a depth and height and breadth and length of moral worth and sanctity, which defies equally the full grasp of thought and of language; but we can understand something of it, and therefore has it been revealed to us. But does it not mark in most fearful contrast the difference which exists between the mind of God and the mind of man? Whilst man is making a mock at sin, God descends from the throne of glory, and takes on him the frailty of a creature, and dies as a creature, the representative of sinners, before his holy nature can pronounce sin forgiven. It was to remove this difference that these glad tidings have been preached; and he that believes this history of God shall be like him, for in it he sees God as he is. In this wonderful transaction, mercy and truth meet together, righteousness and peace embrace each other. It was planned and executed, in order that God might be just whilst he justified the believer in Jesus. It proclaims glory to God in the highest, peace on earth and good-will to man. The new and divinely constituted Head of the human family has been raised from the dead, his sacrifice has been judicially accepted, and he has been crowned with immortality in his representative character. This is the foundation on which sinners are invited to rest the interests of their souls for eternity. It is held up for their most scrutinising inspection, and they are urged to draw near and examine whether it be sufficient to bear their weight. They are asked, as it were, if they can discover a flaw in the fulness and sincerity and efficiency of that love which could prompt God to veil his majesty, and ally himself with our polluted race; and assume an elder brother's interest in our welfare, and magnify the law which we had broken, by suffering its penalty in our room, and thus connect the Divine glory with the salvation of sinners. They are assured on the authority of God, that the blood of Christ cleanseth from all sin, and that there is no condemnation to those who believe on him. They have thus the declaration of God, and the act of God, still more impressive and persuasive than his declaration, to engage their confidence and to banish all doubts and suspicions from their breasts. As the Saviour expired on the cross, he said, "It is finished." The work of expiation was then accomplished: and the history of that work comes forth in the form of a general address to the sons of men, "Return unto me, for I have redeemed you," "Be ye reconciled to God." This is the fountain of the river of life, and over it are these words written, "Ho, every one that thirsteth, come ye to the waters." It proclaims pardon for sin; it is therefore quite suited for sinners. Jesus came not to call the righteous, but sinners to repentance; he came to seek and to save that which was lost. He said this himself, and he said it whilst every possible variety and aggravation of guilt stood full in the view of his omniscience. He said it whilst he was contemplating that cup of bitterness and amazement and death which he had engaged to drink, and which was mixed for him to this very end, that the chief of sinners might be welcomed to the water of life. What is that weight of guilt which can exclude from mercy? The very thought is degrading to the dignity of the sacrifice, and injurious to the holy love which appointed it, and to the unstained truth which has pronounced its all-sufficiency. Can we wonder, then, at the high-toned triumph which filled the soul of the Apostle Paul as he gazed on this glorious object, and saw in it the pledge that his sins, which were many, were forgiven him, and that the heart of his often outraged Master yearned upon him, and that his own lot for eternity was bound up with the glorious eternity of his God? "Who shall lay anything to the charge of God's elect? It is God that justifieth, who is he that condemneth? It is Christ that died, yea, rather that is risen again, who is even at the right hand of God, who also maketh intercession for us."

But if the virtue and sufficiency of the atonement be thus universal, why are not the benefits of it universally enjoyed? Had the mere removal of an impending penalty, in consistency with justice, constituted the whole and the ultimate object of God in this great work, there would probably have been no difference nor individual peculiarity with respect to these benefits, nor should we have had such admonitions addressed to us as the following: "Many are called, but few are chosen;" "work out your own salvation with fear and trembling;" "do all diligence to make your calling and election sure." But Christ gave himself for us, not only to redeem us from the punishment due to iniquity, but also that he might purify to himself a peculiar people, zealous of good works. The subjects of his kingdom were to be those in whose hearts *the truth* dwelt, the great truth relating to the character of God. This truth was developed and exhibited in the atonement,—its bright rays were concentrated there; and therefore the intelligent belief of the atonement was the most proper channel through which this divine light might enter the soul of man. It is this light alone which can chase away the shades of moral darkness, and restore life and spiritual vigour to the numbed and bewildered faculties. And therefore the benefits of the atonement are connected with a belief of the atonement. "He that believeth shall be saved: he that believeth not shall be condemned." When the identity of unhappiness and moral darkness in an intelligent subject of God's government is fully understood, this connection between belief and salvation will appear to be, not the appointment of a new enactment, but merely the renewed declaration of an established and necessary constitution. The truth concerning God's character is an immortal and glorious principle, developed and laid up in Jesus Christ; and God imparts its immortality and glory to the spirits in which it dwells. This truth cannot dwell in us, except in so far as the work of Christ remains as a reality in our minds. We cannot enjoy the spiritual life and peace of the atonement, separated from the believing remembrance of the atonement, as we cannot enjoy the light of the sun separated from the presence of the sun. It would be a foolish madness to think of locking in the light by shutting our casements; and it is no less foolish to dream of appropriating the peace of the Gospel whilst the great truth of the Gospel is not in the eye of faith. In the Epistle to the Galatians (v. 25), St. Paul says, If ye have your life from the Gospel (here called the Spirit), see that you walk in, *i.e.* keep close to, the Gospel. When our hearts stray from the truth, we stray from that life which is contained in the truth. We cannot long continue to retain any moral impression on our minds separate from the object which is fitted to produce the impression.

The man who sees in the atonement a deliverance from ruin and a pledge of immortal bliss, will rejoice in it, and in all the principles which it develops. "Let not the wise man," says the prophet, "glory or rejoice in his wisdom, neither let the mighty man rejoice in his might, let not the rich man rejoice in his riches; but let him that rejoiceth, rejoice in this, that he understandeth and knoweth me, that I am the Lord which exercise loving-kindness, judgment, and righteousness in the earth; for in these things I delight, saith the Lord." He therefore who rejoices in the atonement rejoices in that which delights the heart of God; for here have his loving-kindness, and his judgment, and his righteousness been most fully and most gloriously exercised. It is thus that the believer has communion with God through Jesus Christ, and it is thus that he becomes conformed to his moral likeness. The same truth which gives peace produces also holiness. What a view does the cross of Christ give of the depravity of man and of the guilt of sin! and must not the abhorrence of it be increased tenfold by the consideration that it has been committed against the God of all grace and of all consolation? A sense of our interest would keep us close to that Saviour, in whom our life is treasured up, if we needed such a motive to bind us to a benefactor who chose to bear the wrath of Omnipotence rather than that we should bear it. Shall we frustrate the designs of love by our own undoing, and trample on that sacred blood which was shed for us?

No; if we believe in the atonement, we must love him who made the atonement; and if we love him we shall enter into his views, we shall feel for the honour of God, we shall feel for the souls of men, we shall loathe sin especially in our own hearts, we shall look forward with an earnestness of expectation to the period when the mystery of God shall be finished, and the spiritual temple completed, and the Redeemer's triumph fulfilled. This hope we have as an anchor of the soul, sure and steadfast; it is fixed within the veil; it looks to the atonement; and whatever be the afflictions or the trials of life, it can still rejoice in that voice which whispers from the inner sanctuary, "Be of good cheer, it is I, be not afraid;" it can still feel the force of that reasoning, "He that spared not his own Son, but gave him up for us all, how shall he not with him also freely give us all things?" This hope maketh not ashamed, it will not and cannot disappoint, because it is founded on the character of that God who changeth not.

It is thus that the faith of the Gospel produces that revolution in the mind which is called in Scripture conversion, or the new birth. A man naturally trusts to something within himself, to his prudence, or to his good fortune, or to his worth, or to his acquirements, or to what he has done well, or to his unfeigned sorrow for what he has done ill; self, in one form or other more or less amiable, is the foundation of his hope, and by necessary consequence, self is ever present to his view, and becomes the ultimate object of his conduct, and the director and the former of his character. But when he believes and understands the truth of God as manifested in the atonement, to be the only foundation on which he can rest with safety, the only refuge from that ruin into which he has been led by the guidance of self, he will cast from him these perishing and fluctuating delusions, and he will repose his interests for time and for eternity on the love of him who bled for him, and on the faithfulness of him who is not a man that he should lie, nor the son of a man that he should repent; and resting thus on the character of God as the exclusive ground of his confidence, he will contemplate it as his ultimate object, he will cleave to it as his counsellor and his guide, and will thus be gradually moulded into its likeness.

This foundation of hope continues the same through every stage of the Christian's progress. Though his growth in personal sanctity be the grand and blessed result of his faith, yet that sanctity can never become the ground of his confidence without throwing him back upon self, and separating him from God, and cutting off his supply from the living fountain of holiness, and thus unsanctifying him. But although personal sanctity can never become the foundation of hope, yet it will much strengthen our confidence in that foundation; just as returning health strengthens the confidence of the patient in that medicine which he feels restoring him.

It is a law of our moral constitution, that the foundation of our confidence becomes necessarily the mould of our characters. The principles developed in the atonement are an assemblage of all that is lovely and noble and admirable in spiritual excellence. He, then, that truly and exclusively rests his hope on the atonement becomes a partaker of the character of God. The great argument for the truth of Christianity lies in the sanctifying influence of its doctrines; and alas! the great argument against it lies in the unsanctified lives of its professors. A false exhibition of Christianity is thus more pernicious and more hateful than professed infidelity. But false pretences are not confined to religion; and that man is indeed a fool who throws away his soul because another man is a hypocrite. The Gospel claims and deserves an examination on its own merits, and well will it repay the candid examiner. It warns of a danger, the reality of which is inseparably connected with the admitted holiness of God and the admitted sinfulness of man; it discovers a refuge from this danger, which most beautifully harmonises with all the Divine perfections; and when that refuge is narrowly considered it is found not only to be a place of safety, but to be the entrance into a holy and blessed and glorious immortality. Like the Upas tree, it invites the weary and heavy-laden to its shelter; but, unlike the Upas tree, it dispels their languor, and restores their fainting spirits, and gives a new and a vigorous and an enlivening impulse to every organ of their debilitated frames; its leaves are for the healing of the nations, and its fruit is the bread of life.

Let us now return to the questions with which we commenced these observations, viz., What view does this doctrine give of the character of God? and What influence is the belief of it fitted to exercise on the character of man? and let us, from the statement which has been given, draw out the answers. Love surpassing thought is certainly the prominent feature of that glorious character which is exhibited to us in the atonement;—but it is a love in perfect consistency with a holiness which cannot look upon iniquity,—it is the love of the almighty God, who has not exerted his omnipotence in silencing or overstepping the claims of justice, but in meeting them and fulfilling them. It is a love which sits enthroned on that mercy-seat which rests on eternal truth, and whose very nature it is to hate all evil. The effect upon the character of man, produced by the belief of it, will be to love Him who first loved us, and to put the fullest confidence in his goodness and willingness to forgive—to associate sin with the ideas both of the deepest misery and the basest ingratitude—to admire the unsearchable wisdom and the high principle which have combined the fullest mercy with the most uncompromising justice—and to love all our fellow-creatures from the consideration that our common Father has taken such an interest in their welfare, and from the thought that as we have been all shipwrecked in the same sea by the same wide-wasting tempest, so we are all invited by the same gracious voice to take refuge in the same haven of eternal rest.

It might seem scarcely possible that this simple doctrine should be misapprehended; and yet, from the unaccountable and most unfortunate propensity to look for religious information anywhere rather than in the Bible, it has been perverted in a variety of ways according to the tempers of those who have speculated on it. It has been sometimes so incautiously stated, as to give ground to cavillers for the charge that the Christian scheme represents God's attribute of justice as utterly at variance with every moral principle. The allegation has assumed a form somewhat resembling this, " that according to Christianity, God indeed apportions to every instance and degree of transgression its proper punishment; but that, while he rigidly exacts this punishment, he is not much concerned whether the person who pays it be the real criminal or an innocent being, provided only that it is a full equivalent; nay, that he is under a strange necessity to cancel guilt whenever this equivalent of punishment is tendered to him by whatever hand." This perversion has arisen from the habit amongst some writers on religion of pressing too far the analogy between a crime and a pecuniary debt. It is not surprising that any one who entertains such a view of the subject, should reject Christianity as a revelation of the God of holiness and goodness. But this is not the view given in the Bible. The account which the Bible gives of the matter is this, " Herein is love,— not that we loved God, but that God loved us, and sent his Son to be a propitiation for our sins;" and God set forth Jesus Christ, "to declare his righteousness." Any view of the doctrine which is inconsistent with this account is a perversion of Scripture, for which the perverters are themselves responsible, and not the Bible. The error consists in separating the actions of God from the intention manifested in them towards men. Were such a view, however, of the Divine Being, as that which has been just mentioned, actually and fully believed by any man of an ordinary construction of mind, it would assuredly produce very strange and very melancholy results. He would learn from it to consider the connection between sin and misery, not as a necessary connection, but as an arbitrary one, which might be dissolved, and had been dissolved by the authority of mere power. Thus he could not identify in his thoughts and feelings misery with sin,—which is one of the prominent lessons of the Bible. He could see nothing in the character of God either venerable or lovely. And even the restraint of fear would be removed by the idea, that a penalty had been already paid of greater price than any debt of crime which he had contracted, or could contract. His heart could find in this doctrine no constraining power urging him to the fulfilment of the great commandments of love to God and man. In fact, this doctrine undermines the divinity of Christ as much as Socinianism, inasmuch as it makes a separation between the views and character of the Father and those of the Son.

There is another view of this doctrine, which, though less revolting to the feelings than that which I have just stated, is quite as inconsistent with reason. According to it, the atonement is a scheme by which God has mitigated the strict purity of his law ; so that those who live under the gospel are merely required to yield an imperfect but sincere obedience, instead of that perfect obedience to which they were bound before they professed the faith of Christ. Now, let it be remembered that the love of God *with all the heart* constitutes the substance of the law which we are called on to obey ; and let it also be remembered that the sacrifice of Christ was made not only as a vindication of God's justice in proclaiming pardon to the guilty, but also for the purpose of presenting to the human heart an object most worthy and most admirably fitted to attract all its love : and then it will appear that those who give this interpretation of the doctrine, do in fact maintain that God dispenses with our giving him our full love, on condition *that we are convinced that he deserves this full love at our hands.* The whole end and scope of religion is lost sight of in this interpretation. *Christ gave himself for us, to redeem us from all iniquity, and to purify to himself a peculiar people zealous of good works.* A perfect conformity to the will of God is not only perfect obedience—it is also perfect happiness; and that gracious Father who calls on his creatures to be holy as he is holy, calls on them, by the very same exhortation, to be happy as he is happy. To dispense with our obedience is not mercy to us; for it is in truth to dispense with our happiness. We are not received into the favour of God at all on the ground of our own deservings, but on the ground of the satisfaction made to Divine justice by the death of Christ as the representative of sinners; and the belief of this mercy, by its natural operation, gradually subdues the heart to the love and the obedience of God. Perfect obedience, then, though it is required, and though it is indispensable to perfect happiness, is not the foundation of our hope for eternity. It is the object of our hope, not the foundation of it. We must be trained up to it by the faith of the gospel. It is never attained here in its blessed fulness; and, therefore, perfect happiness is never attained:

but the seed of it may be attained, and may take root in the heart; and it has an eternity before it, to grow and flourish in. An imperfect but sincere obedience will almost always mean, in the human judgment, that degree of obedience which it is convenient to pay;— and this degree is paid by all men. The real glory of Christianity is thus extinguished, because the standard of moral duty is lowered. True humility can have no place in this system, because we limit our duty by our performance. And gratitude for undeserved mercy is excluded, except that base gratitude which thanks God for permitting us to be unholy. God's mercy is a holy mercy: it pardons, but never sanctions imperfection.

There is another view of this subject, certainly not very uncommon amongst those who call themselves Christians, which is as subversive of the principle and efficiency of the gospel as either of those mentioned above. According to this scheme, it is supposed that our hope before God rests on a ground made up partly of our own obedience, and partly of the atoning efficacy of Christ's sacrifice. The work of the Saviour is thus made a supplement to the deficiencies of human merit; and this supplement is conceived to be added as a sort of reward for diligent obedience. The decent and orderly, and well-behaved member of society is thus considered to have a just, though an undefined, claim to a participation in the benefits of the Redeemer's death, whilst the utterly abandoned and profligate is considered unworthy, in his present state, of approaching the cross of Christ, and is, therefore, recommended to reform, that he may bring himself into a condition which may entitle him to do this with a reasonable hope of acceptance. There is a looseness and a vagueness generally attached to the ideas of that class of nominal believers to which I refer, that makes it difficult to meet or to answer their theories; but I am sure that I may confidently appeal to many, whether the statement which has been given does not bear a very near resemblance to some views of the doctrine of the atonement with which they are well acquainted.

The proper answer to these views, when held by one who really assents to the inspiration of the Bible, is, that they are at direct variance with the Bible. Paul says that justification is declared to be of faith, for this very reason, that it might be *gratuitous*, and that all boasting on the part of man might be excluded, etc.; "not by works of righteousness which we have done, but of his mercy he saved us." And when the Jews, who seemed to have prejudices closely allied to those which we are examining, reproached Christ as the friend of publicans and sinners, he answered them, that his business was with sinners; that "the whole needed not a physician, but they that were sick," and that "he came to seek and to save that which was lost."

According to the revealed record, then, that combination of justice and of mercy which was manifested on the cross, is the exclusive ground of hope before God,— and on this ground every one is invited to rest, in the character of a lost sinner, without delay, and without any fruitless and presumptuous attempts to attain a previous worthiness.

It may appear to some that this is a question rather about words than things; but, in fact, it goes to the very root of the Christian character. Is it not evident that upon this system there can be no true humility? because, as we know that that portion of our hope which rests upon Christ is already fixed, and therefore not liable to change, our attention is naturally and necessarily drawn almost entirely to the remaining portion, which is to be made out by ourselves, and which is therefore liable to be changed. Our own doings and deservings become thus the chief objects of our thought. And, let me ask, what are the moral impressions which such objects are fitted to make on the character? If falsely viewed as really worthy titles to the favour of God, they can produce no impressions but those of self-conceit and self-confidence; and if rightly and truly appreciated, they can produce nothing but apprehension or despair. The beauty of the Christian revelation consists in this, that the same object which gives peace to the conscience produces contrition of heart, and is also the most powerful stimulant to holy and grateful obedience. The work of Christ is the sole ground of hope, and is therefore the chief object of thought; and the impressions emanating from this object sum up the Christian character. If I might venture, on such a subject, to allude to the profane mythology of Greece, I think that an illustration of this might be drawn from the fabled contest between Hercules and Antæus. Antæus was the son of the earth, and whenever he touched the earth, fresh vigour was communicated to him. Those blows, therefore, which he sustained from his adversary, and which in other circumstances would have destroyed him, were to him the means of increasing his strength, because they brought him into nearer contact with the earth, which was the source of his strength. The ground on which he rested was the stimulus of his exertions. When the Christian has apprehensions for his safety, he looks to the ground of his hope, and there he finds not only peace but vigour.

But the whole of this erroneous view of the doctrine rests on a false notion with regard to the purpose of the gospel. The gospel addresses men as rebels diseased by sin, and already condemned. The salvation which it offers is most strikingly explained by the prophet Jeremiah, chap. xxxi. 31, and three following verses. It consists in a spiritual character; "I will put my law in their inward parts, and write it in their hearts;" and the mighty instrument by which this effect is to be accomplished is pointed out in the end of the 34th verse, "*for* I will forgive their iniquity, and I will remember their sin no more." That is, the circumstances and the manner in which this pardon is to be proclaimed shall attract the hearts of men to the love and the obedience of God. Salvation, then, means the holy love of God,—a holy obedience of heart, arising from a belief of that mercy which is proclaimed in the gospel. Salvation and obedience mean precisely the same thing; and it is as absurd to say that a man is saved by obedience, as to say that a man is restored to health by getting well. We are not called on to obey, in order to obtain pardon; but we are called on to believe the proclamation of pardon, in order that we may obey. The gospel is said to be " the power of God unto salvation to every one that believeth;" and why? Because God's method of justification is revealed in it to be by faith (Rom. i. 16, 17). I do believe that many preach a different doctrine, from a notion that the true gospel offer of free unconditional pardon is unfavourable to practical obedience and holiness. But, in fact, there is nothing acknowledged by the Bible to be obedience or holiness which does not spring from the belief of this free, undeserved mercy. The attempt at obedience without this, is a most thankless labour—it is never successful,—and even were it successful, it would be the obedience of the hand and not of the heart. It is as if we chose to move the index of a clock with the finger, instead of winding it up. The language of the gospel is, "You shall be ashamed and confounded, because I am pacified towards you for all your iniquities." This plan of pacification wrought out by God himself, is the great subject of the Bible; and the proclamation of this free pardon is the preaching of the gospel; and he who, in his system of teaching, does not hold this up in its proper pre-eminence, is not a preacher of the gospel of Christ. He lays aside that weapon of ethereal temper which God has chosen out of the armoury of heaven, and which he blessed and sanctified for the destruction of moral evil, and goes forth to encounter the powers of darkness without a single well-grounded hope of success. And I am confident that this same doctrine of free grace, if it could be candidly viewed as a mere abstract question in moral science, would compel the approbation of a true philosopher, and that the compromise or mutilation of it (which is less uncommon than the value of souls would lead us to desire) is not more opposed to the authority of the word of God, than it is to the principles of sound reason.

This subject has been already illustrated by examples drawn from human life. I shall now therefore vary the view of it, by considering it in connection with the rite of sacrifice.

The same truth with regard to the character of God and the condition of man, which is so fully developed in the New Testament, is exhibited also in the Old through an obscurer medium,—a medium of types and shadows and prophecy. When the Messiah was promised to our First Parents, the memory and the principle of the promise were embodied in the institution of sacrifice. Sensible objects were necessary, in order to recal to the thoughts and to explain to the understanding of man the spiritual declarations of God. Under the Jewish economy, this institution was enlarged and diversified; but still it pointed to the same *fact,* and illustrated the same *principle.* The *fact* was, the death of Christ for the sins of the world; the *principle* was, that God is at once just and merciful, and that these attributes of his nature are in joint and harmonious operation. Multitudes, probably both of the Jews and of those who lived before the Mosaic system, recognised in their sacrifices that future salvation which was to be wrought out by the promised seed; but a far greater number must be supposed to have stopped short at the rite, through want of spiritual discernment. When the prefigured *fact* was thus forgotten, let us consider whether the moral *principle* exhibited in the ceremony might not still in some measure be understood, and affect the character of the devout worshipper. The full vindication of God's holiness, and of the truth of his denunciations against sin, could indeed rest only on the sacrifice of the Divine Saviour; but although those who saw this great thing through the types which partially obscured whilst they represented it, could alone receive the full benefits of the institution, shall we think that those who did not enter into the spirit of prophecy were entirely excluded from the operation of its principle, and saw nothing of the Divine character manifested in it? As the prosecution of this inquiry may tend to throw greater light on some views which have been already given, I shall here consider the subject of sacrifice apart altogether from its prophetic import. This view of the matter simply regards those particulars which rendered the rite of sacrifice a fit emblem of the atonement of Christ. When God teaches by emblems, He chooses such emblems as are naturally calculated to impress the principle of the antitype upon our minds. There is then a suitableness in animal sacrifices, to give some idea of that great truth which was so gloriously developed in the work of the Saviour when the fulness of time had arrived. Let us consider, then, wherein consists this suitableness. What is the meaning of a sacrifice? What is the purpose of killing a poor animal, because a man has sinned? Can it be supposed that a wise and good God will in reality make a transference of the guilt of the man to the head of the beast?—Impossible: and it is equally impossible to conceive that God should command His creatures to do a thing which they could not understand, and by which, therefore, their characters could not be benefited. The institution contained a great truth, exhibiting God's character, and affecting man's. The suppliant who came with his sacrifice before God, virtually said, "Thou hast appointed this rite as the form through which thy mercy is declared to sinners: and it is indeed in thy mercy alone that I can hope, for I have deserved this death which I now inflict, as the just reward of my transgressions." Thus the mercy and the holiness of God were both kept in view by this rite; and gratitude and penitence would be impressed to a certain degree on the characters of those whose hearts accompanied their hands in the service. This is just an exhibition of the principle in natural religion, that God is gracious, and worthy of our highest love; and that sin deserves punishment, and is connected with misery. Our gratitude, however, for forgiveness would be just in proportion to our apprehensions of the demerit of sin and the danger connected with it, and also to our idea of the interest which God took in our welfare. The death of an animal was the only measure of the guilt and danger of sin, which these sacrifices exhibited; and forgiveness, which seems an easy thing where there is nothing to fear from the power of the offender, was the only measure of the interest which God had taken in our welfare. Thus, these sacrifices rather inculcated on the worshippers the danger and demerit of sin (and this in no very high degree), than the goodness of God. The animal which was slain was the property of the supliant; and he might feel the loss of it to be a species of atoning penalty, as well as a typical representation of the guilt of sin, which would very much diminish his idea both of God's free mercy, and of the guilt of sin which could be so easily atoned. The sacrifice of a man would have furnished a greater measure of guilt; but it could not have impressed on the mind any stronger conviction of the graciousness of God. If we ascend the scale of being, and suppose an incarnate angel to become the victim, the measure by which we may estimate the guilt of sin increases, to be sure, in a very high degree; but still, there is nothing in such a sacrifice which speaks in unequivocal language of the exceeding goodness of God. Although the sufferings of the angel were considered to be perfectly voluntary, it would not alter the view of God's character. Our gratitude would indeed be called forth by the goodness of the angel; but forgiveness still would seem a cheap and easy thing on the part of God, whose creative fiat could call into existence millions of brighter spirits. That God in human nature should himself become the victim, is a scheme which indeed outstrips all anticipation, and baffles the utmost stretch of our minds when we labour to form an idea of perfect benevolence and perfect holiness; but yet it is the only scheme which can fully meet the double object of strongly attracting our love to God, and at the same time of deeply convincing us of the danger and baseness and ingratitude of sin. This gives us a measure by which we may estimate both the Divine goodness and our own guilt. It is indeed an exhibition of "love which passeth knowledge." But yet, when the conscience comes to be fully enlightened, nothing short of this marvellous exhibition can produce peace. When a man is once thoroughly convinced that sin consists in a choice of the heart different from the will of God, even although that choice does not vent itself in an external action, he must feel that he has accumulated, through the past days of his life, and that he is still daily accumulating, a most fearful weight of guilt. A day of retribution approaches, and he must meet God face to face. A simple declaration of forgiveness on the part of God would certainly in these circumstances be most comforting to him; but still it would be difficult to persuade him that the Holy One who inhabiteth eternity could look with kindness on a being so polluted and so opposite in every respect to himself in moral character. Until this persuasion takes hold of his mind, he can neither enjoy real peace, nor be animated with that grateful love which can alone lead to a more perfect obedience. The surpassing kindness and tenderness demonstrated in the cross of Christ, and the full satisfaction there rendered to his violated law, when understood and believed, must sweep away all doubts and fears with regard to God's disposition towards him, and must awaken in his heart that sentiment of grateful and reverential attachment which is the spiritual seed of the heavenly inheritance. "If, when we were enemies, we were reconciled to God by the death of his Son, much more, being reconciled, we shall be saved" by his living love.

It seems to me, that the scriptural statement of this doctrine is in itself the best answer that can be made to Socinians. If Christ was only an inspired teacher, his death is of very small importance to us; because it gives no demonstration of the kindness of God, and therefore can neither give peace to a troubled conscience, nor excite grateful affection: and also, because it gives no high measure of the guilt and danger of sin, and therefore cannot impress us strongly with a sense of its inherent malignity. We thus lose the whole benefit of Christianity as a *palpable* exhibition of the Divine character, and are thrown back again on the inefficiency and vagueness of abstract principles. In this view likewise, all those passages of Scripture in which our gratitude, our reverential esteem, and our filial confidence, are so triumphantly challenged on the ground of the death of Christ, become empty, unmeaning words: for, if Christ was not God, there is no necessary or natural connection between the belief of his death and the excitement of such sentiments in our hearts towards God; while, on the supposition that he was God, the connection is most distinct and unavoidable. In fact, if Jesus Christ was merely a man, the greatest part of the Bible is mere bombast. To a man who disbelieves the inspiration of the Bible, this of course is no argument. But surely he ought not, in a matter of such unspeakable importance, to reject a doctrine which may be true, without examining it in all its bearings. He ought not to take the account of it upon trust, when he has the record itself to apply to. He is right to reject an absurd statement; but he is wrong to decide without investigation that this absurd statement is contained in the Bible. Let him consult the Bible,—let him consider what this doctrine declares of the character of God, let him trace the natural effects of its belief on the character of man,—let him understand that it expands our ideas of the Divine holiness by the very demonstration which attracts our love, that it quickens the sensitiveness of conscience by the very demonstration which gives peace to the conscience,—and he may continue to reject it; but he will not deny that there is a reasonableness in it—that it contains all the elements of a perfect doctrine—that it is most glorifying to God and most suitable to man. To sum up my observations on this subject: The doctrine of the atonement, by the incarnation and death of Christ, is illustrative of the Divine mercy, and vindicative of the Divine holiness; it is a foundation of hope before God, amply sufficient for the most guilty of men; and it is fitted to implant in the vilest heart which will receive it, the principles of true penitence and true gratitude, of ardent attachment to the holy character of God, and of a cordial devotion to his will.

The hallowed purpose of restoring men to the lost image of their Creator, is in fact the very soul and spirit of the Bible; and whenever this object does not distinctly appear, the whole system becomes dead and useless. In creeds and confessions this great purpose is not made to stand forth with its real prominency; its intimate connection with the different articles of faith is not adverted to; the point of the whole argument is thus lost, and

Christianity is misapprehended to be a mere list of mysterious facts. One who understands the Bible may read them with profit, because his own mind may fill up the deficiencies; and when their statements are correct, they may assist inquirers in certain stages, by bringing under their eye a concentrated view of all the points of Christian doctrine, and they may serve, according to their contents, either as public invitations to their communion, or as public warnings against it, and they may stand as doctrinal landmarks; but they are not calculated to impress on the mind of a learner a vivid and useful apprehension of Christianity. The object in them is not to teach religion, but to defend it; and whilst they keep their own place, they are beneficial. But any person who draws his knowledge of the Christian doctrines exclusively or principally from such sources, must run considerable risk of losing the benefit of them, by overlooking their moral objects; and, in so doing, he may be tempted to reject them altogether, because he will be blind to their strongest evidence, which consists in their perfect adaptation to these objects. The Bible is the only perfectly pure source of Divine knowledge; and the man who is unacquainted with it, is in fact ignorant of the doctrines of Christianity, however well read he may be in the schemes and systems and controversies which have been written on the subject.

The habit of viewing the Christian doctrines and the Christian character as two separate things, has a most pernicious tendency. A man who, in his scheme of Christianity, says, "Here are so many things to be believed, and here are so many to be done," has already made a fundamental mistake. The doctrines are the principles which must excite and animate the performance. They are the points from which the lines of conduct flow; and as lines may be supposed to be formed by the progress of their points, or to be drawn out of their substance, so the line of Christian conduct is only formed by the progressive action of Christian principle, or is drawn out of its substance.

The doctrines of revelation form a great spiritual mould, fitted by Divine wisdom for impressing the stamp of the Christian character on the minds that receive them. I shall here mention some of the leading features of that character, as connected with the corresponding doctrines.

The love of God is the radical principle of the Christian character; and to implant this principle is the grand object and the distinct tendency of the Christian doctrines. And it may be proper here to repeat an observation which has been already much insisted on,—that this love is not a vague affection for an ill-defined object, but a sentiment of approbation and attachment to a distinctly-defined character. The Bible calls us to the exercise of this affection, by setting before us a history of the unspeakable mercy of God towards man. At first sight, it might seem impossible to conceive any way in which the mercy of God could be very strikingly or affectingly manifested towards his creatures. His omnipotence and unbounded sovereignty make every imaginable gift cheap and easy to him. The pardon of the sins committed by such feeble worms, seems no great stretch of compassion in so great and so unassailable a Monarch. God knew the heart of man. He knew that such would be his reasonings; and he prepared a work of mercy, which might in all points meet these conceptions. God so loved the world, that he gave his only begotten Son for its salvation. His was not the benevolence which gives an unmissed mite out of a boundless store,—it was a self-sacrificing benevolence, which is but meagrely shadowed forth by any earthly comparison. We admire Codrus sacrificing his life for his country; we admire the guide plunging into the quicksand to warn and save his companions; we admire the father suffering the sentence of his own law in the stead of his son; we admire Regulus submitting to voluntary torture for the glory of Rome: but the goodness of God, in becoming man, and suffering, the just for the unjust, that he might demonstrate to them the evil of sin,—that he might attract their affections to his own character, and thus induce them to follow him in the way of happiness,—was a goodness as much superior to any human goodness, as God is above man, or as the eternal happiness of the soul is above this fleeting existence; and, if believed, must excite a proportionate degree of admiration and gratitude.

The active and cordial love of our fellow-creatures is the second Christian duty. And can this sentiment be more powerfully impressed upon us than by the fact that Christ's blood was shed for them as well as for ourselves; and by the consideration that this blood reproaches us with the basest ingratitude, when we feel or act maliciously, or even slightingly, towards those in whom our heavenly Benefactor took so deep an interest? Under the sense of our Lord's continual presence, we shall endeavour to promote even their temporal welfare; but above all, we shall be earnest for the good of their souls, which he died to redeem.

Christians are commanded to mortify the earthly and selfish passions of ambition and avarice and sensuality. Our Lord died that he might redeem us from such base thraldom, and allure us to the pure liberty of the sons of God. The lust of the flesh, the lust of the eye, and the pride of life, were in fact his murderers. If we love *him*, we must hate *them*, if we love our own peace, we must hate them: for they separate the soul from the Prince of Peace. The happiness of eternity consists in a conformity to the God of holiness; and shall we spend our few days in confirming ourselves in habits directly opposed to him?—No; rather let us begin heaven below, by beginning to be holy.

The Gospel exhorts us to humility; and deep humility, indeed, must be the result of a true acquiescence in the judgment which God passed upon us when he condemned his Son as the representative of our race. And when we think of what our Almighty Father hath done for us, our hearts must often convict us of the strange contrast which is exhibited betwixt our dealings with him and his dealings with us.

We are commanded to be diligent in the duties of life, and to be patient under its sufferings. And to enforce this precept, we are instructed that the minutest event of life is ordered by him who loved us and gave himself for us: and that all these events, how trifling or how calamitous soever they may appear, are yet necessary parts of a great plan of spiritual education, by which he trains his people to his own likeness, and fits them for their heavenly inheritance. He walked himself by the same road—only it was rougher; and he hath shown us by his example, that the cross is a step to glory.

The Scriptures teach that the sentence of death falls upon all mankind, in consequence of the transgression of the first individual; and that eternal life is bestowed on account of the perfect obedience of Jesus Christ. The grand moral purpose for which this doctrine is introduced, is to impress upon our minds a sense of the punishment due to transgression, —of the exceeding opposition which exists between sin and happiness, and of the exceeding harmony which subsists between perfect holiness and eternal glory. The death of a single individual could give no adequate manifestation of the pernicious nature of sin. Death appears sometimes rather as a blessing than an evil; and in general no moral lesson is received from it, except the vanity of earthly things. But when a single offence is presented to us, and there is appended to it the extinction of a whole race as its legitimate consequence, we cannot evade the conviction of its inherent malignity. As the value of this lesson, if really received, infinitely overbalances in the accounts of eternity the loss of this brief mode of our existence, there can be no just ground of complaint against the great Disposer of all things.

In the same way, the hope of eternal life through the obedience of Christ, suggests to us the idea of the strong love and approbation which God feels for moral perfection, and the indissoluble connection in the nature of things between happiness and holiness.

The Divine government in this respect is just a vivid expression of the great moral attribute of God, "that he loveth righteousness, and hateth iniquity." A simple pardon, bestowed without any accompanying circumstances, must have drawn some degree of gratitude from the criminal, if he knew his danger; and this would have been all: but when he views the perfect and holy obedience of a great benefactor as the ground of his pardon, he is induced to look with love and admiration towards that obedience which gained the Divine favour, as well as towards the friend who paid it. A feeling of humble and affectionate dependence on the Saviour, a dread and hatred of sin, and a desire after holiness, are the natural fruits of the belief of this doctrine.

That plan of the Divine government by which God deals with men through a representative, occupies an important place in revealed religion. In the observations which I have here made on this subject, as well as through the whole course of the Treatise, I have in a great measure confined my remarks to the direct connection which subsists between the doctrines of the Bible, and the character which the belief of them is fitted to produce in the mind of man: and with this view I have called the attention of the reader principally to the superiority in real efficiency, which palpable facts, as illustrative of moral principles, possess over a statement of the same principles when in an unembodied and abstract form. But I should be doing a real injury to the cause which I wish to advocate, were I to be the means of conducting any one to the conclusion that Christianity is nothing more than a beautiful piece of moral mechanism, or that its doctrines are mere typical emblems of the moral principles in the Divine mind, well adapted to the understandings and feelings of men. Supposing the history of Codrus to be true, he was under a moral necessity to act as he did, independently of any intention to infuse the spirit of patriotism into his countrymen; and, supposing the Bible to be true, God was under the moral necessity of his own character, to act as he is there represented to have done. The acts there ascribed to him are real acts, not parabolical pictures: they were not only fitted and intended to impress the minds of his creatures—they were also the necessary results and the true vindications of his own character. This belief is inseparably connected with a belief of the reality of Christ's sufferings; and if Christ's sufferings were not real, we may give up the Bible. These sufferings are the foundation of a Christian's hope before God, not only because he sees in them a most marvellous proof of the Divine love, but also because he sees in them the sufferings of the representative of sinners. He sees the denunciations of the law fulfilled, and the bitter cup of indignation allotted to apostasy drained to the very dregs; and he thus perceives that God is just even when justifying the guilty. The identity of the Judge and of the victim dispels the misty ideas of blind vindictiveness with which this scheme may sometimes have been perversely enveloped; and he approaches God with the humble yet confident assurance that he will favourably receive all who come to him in the name of Christ. Whilst he continues in this world, he will remember that the link which binds heaven and earth together is unbroken, and that his great Representative does not in the midst of glory forget what he felt when he was a man of sorrows below. This relation to the Saviour will spiritualise the affections of the believer, and raise him above the afflictions of mortality; and will produce in him a conformity to the character of Christ, which is another name for the happiness of heaven.

I have hitherto been considering the Christian doctrines chiefly as facts embodying the principles of the Divine character; but this spiritual union with the Saviour, as the head and representative of his people, gives to his religion a deeper interest and a sublimer and a more unearthly character than could be excited or expressed by the highest views of holy and gracious worth, even in its more glorious and most lovely operation. We know something of what his official employment is in the sanctuary above; we know something of his glory and of his joy: and shall we not, even in this vale of tears, endeavour to enter into his holy desires, and sympathise with his affections, and triumph in his universal dominion?—He once suffered for us—He now reigns for us. His people were once represented on the cross at Calvary, and they are now represented on the throne of heaven.

The doctrine of the Holy Spirit is also connected with most important moral consequences. He is represented as dictating originally the revealed Word, and as still watching and assisting its progress. He is where the truth is, and he dwells in the hearts where it operates. The general idea of the omnipresence of God is chiefly connected with the belief of his providence and protection, his approving or condemning; but the doctrine of the Spirit is connected in the minds of Christians simply with a belief of his accompanying and giving weight and authority to revealed truth. The truth becomes thus closely associated in their minds with a sense of the presence and the gracious solicitude of God.

With regard to the mode of the operation

of the Holy Spirit on the human mind, the Bible says nothing;—it simply testifies the fact. To this Divine agent we are directed to apply, for the enlightening of the eyes of our understanding, for strength in the inner man, and for all the Christian qualities. These effects are in other places of Scripture referred to the influence of revealed truth itself. We are also told that the Spirit takes of the things relating to Christ and presents them to the soul. We may gather from this, that the Spirit never acts, except through the medium of the doctrines of the Bible. He uses them as instruments naturally fitted for the work. He does not produce the love of God except by the instrumentality of that Divine truth which testifies of the moral excellency and kindness of God. He does not produce humility but through the medium of that truth which declares the extent and spirituality of the requirements of God's law. This doctrine, then, does not in the slightest degree invalidate the argument in favour of revelation, which has been deduced from the natural connection between believing its doctrines and obeying its precepts. These doctrines would of themselves persuade and sanctify a spirit which was not by inclination opposed to their tendency. This Divine agent does not excite feelings or emotions in the mind independent of reason or an intelligible cause. The whole matter of the Bible is addressed to the reason, and its doctrines are intelligible causes of certain moral effects on the characters of those who believe them. The Spirit of God brings these causes to act upon the mind with their natural innate power. This influence, then, is quite different from that inspiration by which prophets were enabled to declare future events. It is an influence which probably can never be distinguished, in our consciousness, from the innate influence of argument or motive. A firm-minded man, unused to the melting mood, may on a particular occasion be moved and excited by a tale of woe far beyond his common state of feeling: his friends may wonder at an agitation so unusual; they may ask him how this story has affected him more than other stories of a similar nature; but he will not be able to give any other reason than what is contained in the distressing facts to which he had been listening. His greater susceptibility in this instance might have originated from some change in his bodily temperament, or from certain trains of thought which had previously been passing through his mind: but these circumstances did not make the impression; they only made him more fit to receive the impression from an object which was naturally calculated to make it. The impression was entirely made by the story,—just as the impression upon wax is entirely made by the seal, although heat may be required to fit it for receiving the impression.

I have used this illustration to show that the influence of the Spirit does not necessarily destroy, and is not necessarily independent of, that natural relation of cause and effect which subsists between the doctrines taught and the moral character recommended by the Bible.

When the prophet Elisha was surrounded in Dothan by the Syrian army, he felt no fear, because he placed full confidence in the protection of God. But his servant was terrified by the appearance of inevitable ruin. It pleased God, however, to deliver him at once from his agitation and perplexity, even before he thought fit to remove the appearance of the danger. And how was this effected? "God opened the young man's eyes, and he saw: and, behold, the mountain was full of horses and chariots of fire round about Elisha." God here interposed miraculously, in order to calm the man's spirit. But mark the nature of the interposition; God dealt with the man as a reasonable being,—he gave him ocular demonstration of his safety. He did not work in his mind an unaccountable intrepidity in the face of danger which *he* could not have explained, but discovered to him a fact, which, from the nature of the human mind, could not fail of dispelling his fearful apprehensions. Had he given full credit to the assurances of his master, his mind would have been at peace without the interposition of this supernatural revelation. But although he acknowledged his master to be a prophet, yet he did not place that implicit reliance on his testimony which was sufficient to overcome the violent excitement produced in his mind by the visible objects of terror which surrounded him. When his eyes were opened, he saw and believed; and this belief brought peace.

It was not the miraculous interposition abstractly, which produced this effect; it was the glorious army of guardian angels, miraculously unveiled to his eye, which inspired him with confidence, and enabled him to despise the Syrian power. If, instead of these friendly hosts, he had seen the angel whom David saw with a sword drawn over Jerusalem, the sight would only have increased his alarm. It is then the object believed, from whatever source the belief proceeds, whether from seeing or hearing, which operates on the mind.

That the belief of the gospel is in every instance the work of the Holy Spirit, no one who believes in the Bible can doubt; and indeed this doctrine is the ground of the Christian's confidence that he shall continue steadfast unto the end. But still it must be remembered that it is not the supernatural agency itself abstractly which gives Christian peace and Christian strength to the mind, but the history of the Saviour's work, which through this medium is spiritually revealed to it. The Lord opened the heart of Lydia to attend to the things spoken by Paul. If our notions of

Divine influence lead us away from attending to the things contained in the gospel, we are deluding ourselves. And on the other hand, if our mode of studying the Bible does not cultivate in us a conviction of our own weakness, and an habitual dependence on the operations of the Holy Spirit, we certainly do not belong to that society who are said to be "all taught of God," and we have no spiritual discernment of the truth. When we study the doctrines of revelation, we ought to study them in that connection in which they stand in the Bible itself. They are not given to us for the purpose of exercising our faculties in speculative discussion, but for practical usefulness. The observance of this rule will save us from much perplexity, and many a thorny and agitating question. In the Bible, this doctrine of Divine influence which we are now considering, is uniformly connected with the most explicit declarations that man is free to act, and responsible for his actions. Man's inability to obey God consists absolutely in his unwillingness, and is but another name for the greatest degree of this. There is nothing to prevent him from embracing the gospel, and walking in the ways of holiness, but his own opposite inclinations. "This is the condemnation, that light is come into the world, and men have loved darkness rather than light, because their deeds are evil" (John iii. 19). It is worthy of remark that our Lord makes this statement in that very conversation in which he insists on the necessity under which every individual lies of being spiritually born again before he can enter the kingdom of God. In the gospel, sinners are called upon, not to be supernaturally influenced, but to believe the Divine testimony. And the question at last will be, not by what influence or arguments were you led to the Saviour, but, did you embrace his offered salvation? It is not very uncommon to hear religious persons speak of faith and holiness merely as evidences of a Divine operation on the heart, and as valuable simply on this account. But such language is not borrowed from the Scriptures. Here we find faith and holiness considered as qualities valuable in themselves, and as duties imperative on all to whom the message is published. "Repent (*i.e.* change your principles) and believe the gospel," is the substance of the first discourse preached, after the ascension of our Lord, to his very murderers. And this same exhortation is thrown loose upon the world, and, when rejected, is rejected wilfully and at the peril of the rejectors. The evidences for the gospel, both external and internal, are suited to the human faculties; and so too is the substance of its contents. A sinner who admits its evidence, and who reads it with the attention which such an admission demands, and who finds in it peace to his conscience and good hope for eternity, through the great atonement, will assuredly, if he has indeed made this happy discovery, acknowledge with humility and gratitude the kindness of God in leading him out of darkness into this marvellous light; and he will continue to look to that Divine and unseen influence, which first stopped him in his downward course, for support and encouragement during the remainder of his pilgrimage. And he who is condemned for rejecting the gospel will be condemned on this ground, viz., that he might, as well as ought to have done otherwise; and that he has resisted the conviction both of his reason and conscience, which had testified against him. It is our duty and our privilege to look to the free offer of salvation, and the sufficiency of the atonement; and we are wandering from the Bible, and from peace, and from piety, when we occupy our thoughts with such difficulties.

But why was this doctrine revealed, and what benefit is to be derived from believing it? What effect is the belief of it calculated to produce on our characters; and what light does it throw on the character of God, or on the condition of man? As the work of the Spirit is to enlighten the eyes of our understanding with regard to Divine truth, and to take of the things of Christ and show them to us, the belief of this doctrine of course includes the conviction that we stand in need of this light, and that the inclination of our hearts naturally leads us from the things of Christ. This conviction, if real, will humble us before God, and excite us to a jealous vigilance over every motion of our minds. In this doctrine, also, God gives a manifestation of his own character. He presents himself to his weak and ignorant creatures as ready to meet all their wants and supply all their deficiencies; and thus condescends to solicit their confidence. He promises his Spirit to those who ask; and thus invites and stimulates them to hold frequent intercourse with himself by prayer. He declares his holy anxiety for the advancement of the truth; and thus attracts their attention and regard to it.

When the arguments of the gospel alarm or confirm or comfort the mind, the Holy Spirit is present; and the belief of this will unspeakably enforce the argument,—just as we often find that the presence and voice of a friend will give weight to reasons which would be disregarded in his absence. If God thus offers us his spiritual presence and support through the medium of his truth, ought not we ever to carry about with us the remembrance and the love of the truth, that we may enjoy much of his presence and support? If he is so watchful over the progress of Christian principle in the hearts of men, ought not we also to be watchful, lest we grieve him, and lest we lose the precious benefits of his instructions? As the gospel confines the influence of the Spirit to the truths contained in the written Word, there is nothing to fear from fanaticism. The Holy Spirit does not now reveal anything new, but impresses what is already revealed.

SECTION V.

It thus appears that the gospel is a great storehouse of medicines for the moral diseases of the human mind. It contains arguments most correctly fitted to act powerfully on our reason and on our feelings; and these arguments are in themselves naturally destructive of moral evil. They give a life and a reality to the shadowy traits of natural religion; they exhibit in a history of facts the abstract idea of the Divine character; and thus they render that character intelligible to the comprehension, and impressive on the heart of man. And is there no need for this medicine? If it be admitted that wickedness and misery reign in this world to a frightful extent, and that nothing is more common than a strange carelessness about our Creator, and a decided spirit of hostility to the holiness of his character;—if it be admitted that there prevails, through the hearts of our species, a proud selfishness of disposition which looks with indifference on the happiness or misery of others, unless where interest or vanity makes the exception,— and that whilst we profess to believe in a future state, we yet think and act as if our expectations and desires never stretched beyond this scene of transitory existence;—if all this be admitted, surely it must also be admitted that some remedy is most desirable. And when we consider that the root of all these evils is in the heart,—that the very first principles of our moral nature are corrupted,—that the current of our wills is different from that of God's,—and that whilst this difference continues, we must be unhappy, or at best, most insecure of our enjoyment, in whatever region our lot of existence is cast,— the necessity of some powerful health-restoring antidote will appear still more imperious. And can we think it improbable that a gracious God would meet this necessity and reveal this antidote? We have advanced a considerable step when we have admitted this probability. And when we see a system such as Christianity, asserting to itself a Divine original—tending most distinctly to the eradication of moral evil—harmonising so beautifully with the most enlightened views of the character of God, and adapted so wonderfully to the capacities of man,—does not the probability amount to an assurance that God has indeed made a movement towards man, and that such an antidote is indeed contained in thetruth of the gospel?

There are few minds darkened or hardened to such a degree that they cannot discern between moral good and evil. Hence it happens that the pure morality of the gospel is generally talked of with praise; and this is all. They admire the dial-plate and the timepiece, and the accurate division of its circle; whilst they altogether pass over that nice adjustment of springs and weights which give its regulated movement to the index: they see not the Divine wisdom of the doctrines, which can alone embody that pure morality in the characters of those who receive them.

Exactly from the same inadvertence, it is sometimes asked, "Why so urgent with these abstruse and mysterious doctrines? It is, to be sure, very decent and proper to believe them. But the character is the great point; and if that be reformed, we need not care much about the means." These persons do not consider, that though it may be comparatively easy to restrain the more violent eruptions of those dispositions which are mischievous to society, it is no easy matter to plant in the heart the love of God, which is the first and greatest moral precept of Christianity. They do not consider that the character is in the mind; and that this character must receive its denomination of good or bad according as it capacitates its possessor for happiness or misery, when in direct contact with the character of God. The obedience of the will and of the heart is required; and this implies in it a love for those holy principles in which the rule of duty is founded. A mere knowledge of duty, even when joined with a desire to fulfil it, can never inspire this love. We cannot love anything by simply endeavouring to love it. In order to this, we must see somewhat in it which naturally attracts our affections. Whatever this *somewhat* may be, it constitutes the doctrine which forms our characters on that particular subject. This law holds in all such operations of the mind; but most conspicuously does it hold where the natural bent of the inclination takes an opposite course,—as in the case of Christian duty. Duty must be presented to our minds, as associated with circumstances which will call forth our love,—as associated with the impulses of esteem, of gratitude, and interest,—else we can never love it. These circumstances constitute the Christian doctrines; and the reasonableness of continually and closely urging them is founded on that law of the human mind which has been alluded to. It is not easy to cast out pride and self-conceit from the heart, nor to look upon the distresses of life with a cheerful acquiescence in that sovereign will which appoints them. It is not easy for a mind which has been much engrossed by its outward relations to the visible system with which it is connected, to receive and retain a practical impression, that there is, throughout the universe, one great spiritual and invisible dominion, to which all these lesser systems are subservient, and in which they are embraced; and that these are but schools and training seminaries in which immortal spirits are placed, that they may learn to know and to do the will of God. It is not a mere knowledge of duty which will enable us to resist the noxious impressions which are continually emanating from the objects of our senses, and from the relations of life—to disregard the pressing temptations of ambition or indolence, of avarice or sensuality—to expel those worldly anxieties which corrode the soul—and to run the way of God's commandments, through difficulties and dangers, through evil report and good report. These things require a more energetic principle than the knowledge, even when conjoined with the approbation of what is right. The love of God must be rooted in the heart; and this can only be accomplished by habitually viewing him in all the amiableness of his love and of his holiness. We must acquaint ourselves with God; for it is the knowledge of his high character alone which can humble the pride of man, or throw light on the obscurities of his condition here, or call forth that sentiment of devoted love which will stamp the Divine image on his heart; and it is a conformity to that character alone which can make us freemen of the universe, and secure to us tranquillity and joy in every region of creation; because this conformity of character is the living principle of union which pervades and binds together the whole family of God, and capacitates the meanest of its members for partaking in the blessedness of their common Father.

It should be observed, that when conformity to the Divine character is mentioned as the result of a belief of the Christian doctrine, it is very far from being meant that the conformity will be perfect, or that the character will be free from failings, or even considerable faults. All that is meant is, that the principle which will produce a perfect conformity is there. Thus we may say that a child has a conformity to his father's will, if he is strongly attached to him, and is sincerely anxious to please him, although levity or passion may occasionally carry him off from his duty. This is only the budding-time of Christianity; eternity is the clime in which the flower blows. If it were perfected here, there would be no occasion for death,—this world would be heaven.

When we talk of love towards an invisible

being, we evidently mean love to the principles of his character. Love to God, therefore, implies a knowledge of his character; and thus, if in our idea of God, we exclude his holiness and justice and purity, and then give our affection to the remaining fragments of his character, we do not in fact love God, but a creature of our own imagination. It is a love of the whole which can alone produce a resemblance of the whole; and nothing short of this love can produce such a resemblance. If this world bounded our existence, there would be little occasion for these heavenly views; because the order of society can in general be tolerably preserved by human laws and the restraint of human opinion; and for the few years which we have to pass here, this is sufficient: but if we are placed here to become fitted for eternity we must know God, and love him, in order that we may have pleasure in his presence, and in the manifestations of his will.

There is an important part of the subject still untouched, which is intimately connected with the principle of the preceding argument, and is most deserving of a full and minute consideration: I mean the harmony which subsists between the views of the Bible and that system of events which is moving on around us. On this point, however, I shall only make a very few general observations.

If we look on this world as a school in which the principles of the Bible are inculcated and exercised, we shall find that the whole apparatus is admirably fitted for the purpose. As adventures of danger are adapted to exercise and confirm the principle of intrepidity, so the varied events of life are adapted to exercise and confirm the principles of the Christian character. The history of the world, and our own experience of it, present to us as it were a scene of shifting sand, without a single point on which we may reasonably rest the full weight of our hopes with perfect confidence. The gospel presents to us, on the other hand, the unchangeable character of God, and invites us to rest there. The object of our hope becomes the mould of our characters; and happiness consists in a character conformed to that of God. But there is a constant tendency in our minds to occupy themselves with the uncertain and unsatisfactory things which are seen, to the exclusion of that secure good which is unseen. Pain, disappointment, and death, are therefore sent to awaken us to reflection,—to warn us against reposing on a shadow, which will stamp on us its own corruptible and fleeting likeness,—and to invite us to fix our feet on that substantial rock which cannot fail. The happiness which God intends for men (according to the Bible) consists in a particular form of character; and that character can only be wrought out by trials and difficulties and afflictions. If this were practically remembered, it would associate in our minds the sorrows of life with solid happiness and future glory. Every event, of whatever description it be, would appear to us an opportunity of exercising and strengthening some principle which contains in itself the elements of happiness. This consideration would swallow up, or at least very much abate, the dejection or exultation which the external form of the event is calculated to excite, and produce cheerful and composed acquiescence in the appointments of Providence. "In every thing give thanks; for this (event, whether prosperous or adverse) is the will of God in Christ Jesus concerning you." It forms a part of that system of wisdom and love, of which the gift of Christ is the prominent feature and the great specimen. Christ was given to bring men near to God, and every part of the system of Providence is ordered with the same design. The Captain of our salvation was "a man of sorrows, and acquainted with grief;" and whilst his wisdom appoints the medicinal sorrow, his heart sympathises with the sufferer. His sufferings were not only endured in satisfaction of Divine justice,—they also serve as a pattern of the way by which God leads those real sinners whom the sinless Saviour represented, unto holiness. When two of his disciples asked him for the chief places in his kingdom, the nature of which they had much mistaken, he answered them, "Can ye drink of the cup which I drink of, and can ye be baptized with the baptism which I am baptized with?"— thus teaching, that as his own way to glory lay through sorrows, so theirs did also. His road and his glory were the patterns of theirs. Not that happiness and glory are given as an arbitrary premium for having suffered, but that the character which has been most exercised and refined by affliction contains a greater proportion of the constituent elements of happiness and glory. Neither are we to suppose that afflictions necessarily produce this character: indeed, the effect in many cases is the very reverse. But afflictions are important opportunities of acquiring and growing in this character; which, as they cannot be neglected without danger, so they cannot be improved according to the directions of the gospel without leading to a blessed result. The continual presence of God watching over the progress of his own work, and observing the spirit in which his creatures receive their appointed trials, is a great truth, which, if believed and remembered, would both excite to cheerful and grateful action, and would comfort under any sorrow.

Every event affords opportunities of exercising love to God or man, humility, or heavenly-mindedness; and thus every event may be made a step towards heaven: so that, if we were asked what sort of a theatre the principles of the gospel required for its effectual operation on a being like man, it would be impossible to devise any which would appear even to our reason so suitable as the world which we see around us. Were the gospel different, or were men different, another theatre might be better; but whilst the human heart remains as it is, we require just such a process as that which is carried on here, for working the principles of the gospel into our moral constitutions. We know, besides, that the Christian character is adapted to the events of life; because it would produce happiness under those events, whatever they might be. Thus it appears, that the heart of man, the Bible, and the course of Providence, have a mutual adaptation to each other; and hence we may conclude that they proceed from the same source,—we may conclude that the same God who made man, and encompassed him with the trials of life, gave the Bible to instruct him how these trials might be made subservient to his eternal happiness.

The world then is a theatre for exercising and strengthening principles. Its events operate on the moral seeds in the human mind, as the elements of nature, heat, moisture, and air, do on vegetable seeds. They develop their qualities, they foster them into life and energy, they bring forth into full display all their capacities of evil and good; but they do the same office to poisonous and useless seeds as to the most excellent. How careful then ought we to be that the moral principles of our minds should be of the right kind! Poisonous plants are native to the soil, whilst the immortal seed of Divine truth is an exotic, from a more genial clime. But if this course of discipline be so necessary for the growth and conformation of the truth in the heart, then the gospel may appear to be exclusively addressed to those who have a series of years and exercises before them. In what form can it approach a death-bed? What has the Bible to say to a man within an hour of eternity, who has either never heard, or never attended, to the message of peace? In fact, it speaks the same language to him that it does to the youth just entering on the career of life—the same glad tidings are proclaimed to sinners of all ages—of all conditions, and in all circumstances: "This is the testimony, that God hath given to us eternal life, and this life is in his Son."—Although happiness is necessarily connected with, or more properly is identical with, that holiness which the belief of the truth induces; yet pardon and acceptance are not the consequences of a change of character, they are the free gift of God, through Jesus Christ; and that they are so, enters into the very substance of that record which we are called on to believe, as the testimony of God.

The judicial sentence against sin has been executed, and the honour of the Divine law has been vindicated, by a deed of unutterable love, which claims from men the most grateful and reposing confidence in the reality of that mercy, and the inviolableness of that truth which, amidst the agonies of death, declared the work of reconciliation accomplished. The belief of this transaction, if full and perfect, would at once, and instantaneously, change the heart into a conformity with the will of God, which is the character of heaven, without which heaven could be no place of happiness. It is the weakness, the deficiency, and unsettledness of this belief, which makes the transformation of the heart, in general, so tardy a process. The tardiness does not, however, belong to the nature of the truth, but to the mode of its reception. And that Spirit, which is mighty in operation, can open the spiritual eye at the last moment to perceive the excellency of the Saviour, and thus cause the young germ of glory to burst forth at once into full and vigorous life.

Very sudden and unexpected changes of character do sometimes take place in the history of this world's moralities; and it may perhaps assist our conception to adduce an example of this kind in illustration of that higher and more important change which we are at present considering. Mr. Foster, in his Essay on *Decision of Character*, gives an account of a man who, from being a perfect prodigal, became all at once a most beggarly miser. Whilst yet a boy he had come to the possession of a large fortune, and before he was of age he contrived to get rid of it by a course of the most profligate extravagance. After his last shilling was gone, his spirits fell and he went out with a thought of putting an end to his life. Providence directed him to the top of an eminence, from which he could survey every acre which he had so foolishly squandered. Here he sat down, and in bitterness of heart contrasted his former splendour with his present wretchedness. As he viewed his past life, the absurdity of his conduct appeared to him so glaring, and want appeared so frightful, that he was filled with a loathing for everything like expense. He instantly formed the resolution of retracing his steps, and recovering his possessions. He descended the hill a thorough miser, and continued so to his death. The principle of penurious and greedy saving had expelled its opposite, and taken firm hold of his soul; his character was entirely changed, and his future life was only a development of the feeling acquired in that moment.

Now, though the change from one mode of selfishness to another, as in this instance, is a very different thing from the conversion of the heart to God; yet as the change of character in both cases arises from *a real change in the conviction of the mind as to what is truly good* (from whatever sources of influence these convictions may proceed, whether earthly, as in the one case, or heavenly, as in the other), I consider myself entitled to use this analogy as an argument against those who either ridicule sudden conversions as absurd fables, or who confine such events to the miraculous period of

Christianity. Is it rational to suppose that a conviction of the love of God—of the vastness of eternity, of the glory of heaven, of the misery of hell—should be insufficient to produce an instantaneous change of no light nature, when we see so striking a change produced by the comparative prospect of wealth or poverty for a few uncertain years? Shall we suppose that the Spirit of God hath less power than the spirit of Mammon? or, does it belong only to things which pass away to exert a sovereignty over the springs of the mind? And are things which abide for ever to be alone considered as powerless and inefficient? Could we imagine such a thing as *a paradise for misers* under the government of a God who giveth to all men liberally and upbraideth not, we might safely say that if the young man, whose history we have been contemplating, had dropped down dead as he descended from the eminence which had witnessed his resolution, he would have been fit for a situation there. Nor would his former conduct have debarred him from the full enjoyment of its delights. So when the pardoning mercy of God is perceived in its glory and its beauty, it capacitates the mind immediately, however dark and vile before, for that bliss which it so freely bestows, and girds and prepares the parting traveller for that everlasting kingdom of our Lord and Saviour, an entrance into which it so abundantly ministers, even though this may be the first look he has ever cast towards that happy land, and the last look he takes of aught until the body returns to the dust, and the spirit to him who gave it.

The Bible never shuts out hope; and in the example of the thief on the cross it invites the dying sinner to look, that he may live for ever. But the Bible never encourages the negligent, nor the presumptuous—it warns of the uncertainty of life and opportunity, and it exhibits the difficulty of overcoming settled habits of sin, under the similitude of the leopard changing his spots, or the Ethiopian his skin. In truth, every hour of delay makes this change more difficult and improbable,—because every hour is giving growth and strength to principles of an opposite description; he is grieving and despising the Holy Spirit, and is making a dark league with hell, which is gaining validity and ratification by every act in accordance with it.

SECTION VI.

I HAVE already explained two causes why spiritual Christianity is so much opposed, and so rarely received with true cordiality amongst men. The first is, that its uncompromising holiness of principle arms against it all the corruptions of our nature: The second is, that it rarely gains an attentive and full consideration, so as to be apprehended in all its bearings, both in relation to the character of God and its influence on the heart of man.

I shall now mention another circumstance, nearly connected with the second of these causes, which often opposes the progress of true religion.

Many persons, in their speculations on Christianity, never get farther than the miracles which were wrought in confirmation of its Divine authority. Those who reject them are called infidels, and those who admit them are called believers; and yet, after all, there may be very little difference between them. A belief of the miracles narrated in the New Testament does not constitute the faith of a Christian. These miracles merely attest the authority of the messenger,—they are not themselves the message. They are like the patentee's name on a patent medicine, which only attests its genuineness, and refers to the character of its inventor, but does not add to its virtue. Now, if we had such a scientific acquaintance with the general properties of drugs, that from examining them we could predict their effects, then we should, in forming our judgment of a medicine, trust to our own analysis of its component parts, as well as to the inventor's name on the outside; and if the physician whose name it bore was a man of acknowledged eminence in his profession, we should be confirmed in our belief that it was really his invention, and not the imposture of an empiric, by observing that the skill displayed in its composition was worthy of the character of its assigned author, and that it was well suited to the cases which it was proposed to remedy. And even though the name should be somewhat soiled, so as to be with difficulty deciphered, yet if the skill were distinctly legible, we should not hesitate to attribute it to a man of science, nor should we scruple to use it ourselves on its own evidence, if our circumstances required such an application.

If Alexander the Great could, by his own skill, have discovered, in the cup presented to him by Philip, certain natural causes restorative of health, his confidence in the fidelity of his physician would have had a powerful auxiliary in his own knowledge of the subject. The conviction of his friend's integrity was, in his case, however, sufficient by itself to overcome the suspicions of Parmenio. But if, by his own knowledge, he had detected anything in the cup which appeared to him decidedly noxious, his confidence in his friend would have only led him to the conclusion that this cup was really not prepared by him, but that some traitor, unobserved by him, had infused a poisonous ingredient into it.

In like manner, if we discern that harmony in the Christian revelation which is the stamp of God upon it, we shall find little difficulty in admitting that external evidence by which he attested it to the world. And even though our opportunities or acquirements do not qualify us for following the argument in support of miracles, yet if we are convinced that the remedial virtue of its doctrines suits the necessities and diseases of our nature, we will not hesitate to assign it to the Great Physician of souls as its author, nor will we scruple to use it for our own spiritual health.

No one who knows what God is will refuse to receive a system of doctrines which he really believes was communicated by God. But, then, no one in the right exercise of his reason can, by any evidence, be brought to believe that what appears to him an absolute absurdity, did ever in truth come from God. At this point, the importance of the internal evidence of revelation appears most conspicuous. If any intelligent man has, from hasty views of the subject, received the impression that Christianity is an absurdity, or contains absurdities, he is in a condition to examine the most perfect chain of evidence in its support, with the simple feeling of astonishment at the ingenuity and the fallibility of the human understanding.

On a man in this state of mind, all arguments drawn from external evidence are thrown away. The thing which he wants is to know that the subject is worth a demonstration; and this can only be learned by the study of the Bible itself. Let him but give his unprejudiced attention to this book, and he will discover that there is contained in it the development of a mighty scheme admirably fitted for the accomplishment of a mighty purpose: he will discover that this purpose is no less than to impart to man the happiness of God, by conforming him to the character of God: and he will observe with delight and with astonishment, that the grand and simple scheme by which this is accomplished, exhibits a system of moral mechanism, which, by the laws of our mental constitution, has a tendency to produce that character, as directly and necessarily as the belief of danger has to produce alarm, the belief of kindness to produce gratitude, or the belief of worth to produce esteem. He will discern that this moral mechanism bears no mark of imposture or delusion, but consists simply in a manifestation of the moral character of God, accommodated to the understandings and hearts of men. And lastly, he will perceive that this manifestation only gives life and palpability to that vague, though sublime, idea of the Supreme Being, which is suggested by enlightened reason and conscience.

When a man sees all this in the Bible, his sentiment will be, "I shall examine the evidence in support of the miraculous history of this book; and I cannot but hope to find it convincing. But even should I be left unsatisfied as to the continuity of the chain of evidence, yet of one thing I am persuaded,—it has probed the disease of the human heart to the bottom; it has laid bare the source of its aberration from moral good and true happiness; and it has propounded a remedy which carries in itself the proof of its efficiency. The cause seems worthy of the interposition of God. He did once certainly display his own direct and immediate agency in the creation of the world; and shall I deem it inconsistent with his gracious character, that he has made another immediate manifestation of himself in a work which had for its object the restoration of innumerable immortal spirits to that eternal happiness, from which, by their moral depravation, they had excluded themselves?"

The external evidence is strong enough, if duly considered, to convince any man of any fact which he has not in the first place shut out from the common privilege of proof, by pronouncing it to be an impossibility. This idea of impossibility, when attached to the gospel, arises generally, as was before observed, from some mistaken notion respecting the matter contained in it. A very few remarks may be sufficient to show that this is the case. Those who hold this opinion do not mean to say *absolutely* that it is impossible to suppose, in consistency with reason, that God ever would make a direct manifestation of his own immediate agency in any case whatever; because this would be in the very face of their own general acknowledgments with regard to the creation of the world: they must therefore be understood to mean no more than that, considering the object and structure of Christianity, it is unreasonable to suppose that it could be the subject of a direct interposition from Heaven. We are thus brought precisely to the argument which it has been the intention of this Essay to illustrate.

Now, if we suppose that it was one of the objects of the Creator, in the formation of the world, to impress upon his intelligent creatures an idea of his moral character,—or, in other words, to teach them natural religion, (and that it was one of his objects, we may presume, from its having in some measure had this effect,)—it follows, that a direct and immediate agency on the part of God is closely connected with the design of manifesting his moral character to man; and we may expect to meet these two things linked together in the system of God's government. If, therefore, the gospel contains a most vivid and impressive view of the Divine character, harmonising with the revelation of nature, but far exceeding it in fulness and in power, are we to be surprised at an interposition in its behalf of the same agency which was once before exhibited for a similar purpose? Thus, the object of the gospel, and its adaptation to that object, become the great arguments for its truth; and those who have not studied it in this relation are not competent judges of the question. Indeed, if we take the truth of the gospel for granted, we must infer that this distinct and beautiful adaptation of its means to its end was intended by its Divine Author as its chief evidence; since he must have foreseen that not one out of a hundred who should ever hear of it could either have leisure or learning to weigh its external evidence. And this will explain a great deal of infidelity; for freethinkers in general are not acquainted with the substance of revelation; and thus they neglect that very point in it on which God himself rested its probability, and by which he invites belief.

There may be also, for anything that the reasoners of this world know, cycles in the moral world as well as in the natural; there may be certain moral conjunctures, which, by the Divine appointment, call for a manifestation of direct agency from the great First Cause; and in this view a miraculous interposition, though posterior to the creation, cannot be considered as an infringement of the original scheme of things, but as a part, and an essential part of it. When the world was less advanced in natural science than it is at present, a comet was considered an infringement on the original plan. And the period may arrive, and will assuredly arrive, when the spirits of just men made perfect shall discern as necessary a connection between the character of God and all the obscurities of his moral government in our world, as the philosopher now discerns between the properties of matter and the movements of the various bodies belonging to our planetary system.

If the gospel really was a communication from heaven, it was to be expected that it would be ushered into the world by a miraculous attestation. It might have been considered as giving a faithful delineation of the Divine character, although it had not been so attested; but it could never have impressed so deep a conviction, nor have drawn such reverence from the minds of men, had it not been sanctioned by credentials which could come from none other than the King of kings. As this conviction and this reverence were necessary to the accomplishment of its moral object, the miracles which produced them were also necessary. Under the name of miraculous attestations, I mean merely those miracles which were extrinsic to the gospel, and did not form an essential part of it; for the greatest miracles of all—namely, the conception, resurrection, and ascension of our Lord—constitute the very substance of the Divine communication, and are essential to the development of that Divine character which gives to the gospel its whole importance.

The belief of the miraculous attestation of the gospel, then, is just so far useful as it excites our reverence for, and fixes our attention on, the truth contained in the gospel. All the promises of the gospel are to faith in the gospel, and to those moral qualities which faith produces; and we cannot believe that which we do not understand. We may believe that there is more in a thing than we can understand; or we may believe a fact, the causes or modes of which we do not understand; but our actual belief is necessarily limited by our actual understanding. Thus, we understand what we say when we profess our belief that God became man, although we do not understand *how*. This *how*, therefore, is not the subject of belief; because it is not the subject of understanding.

We, however, understand *why,*—namely, that sinners might be saved, and the Divine character made level to our capacities; and therefore this is a subject of belief. In fact, we can as easily remember a thing which we never knew, as believe a thing that we do not understand. In order, then, to believe the gospel, we must understand it; and in order to understand it, we must give it our serious consideration. An admission of the truth of its miraculous attestation, unaccompanied with a knowledge of its principles, serves no other purpose than to give a most mournful example of the extreme levity of the human mind. It is an acknowledgment that the Almighty took such a fatherly interest in the affairs of men, that he made a direct manifestation of himself in this world for their instruction; and yet they feel no concern upon the subject of this instruction. Nevertheless, they say, and perhaps think, that they believe the gospel. One of the miraculous appearances connected with our Saviour's ministry places this matter in a very clear light. When, on the mount of transfiguration, he for a short time anticipated the celestial glory in the presence of three of his disciples, a voice came from heaven saying, "This is my beloved Son; *hear ye him.*" He was sent to tell men something which they did not know. Those, therefore, who believed the reality of this miraculous appearance, and yet did not listen to what he taught, rejected him on the very ground on which it was of prime importance that they should receive him.

The regeneration of the character is the grand object; and this can only be effected by the pressure of the truth upon the mind. Our knowledge of this truth must be accurate, in order that the image impressed upon the heart may be correct; but we must also know it in all the awfulness of its authority, in order that the impression may be deep and lasting. Its motives must be ever operating on us,—its representations ever recurring to us—its hopes ever animating us. This will not relax, but rather increase our diligence in the business of life. When we are engaged in the service of a friend, do we find that the thought of that friend and of his kindness retards our exertions? —No. And when we consider all the business of life as work appointed to us by our Father, we shall be diligent in it for his sake. In fact, however clearly we may be able to state the subject, and however strenuous we may be in all the orthodoxy of its defence, there must be some flaw in our view of it, if it remains only a casual or an uninfluential visitor of our hearts. Its interests are continually pressing: eternity is every moment coming nearer; and our characters are hourly assuming a form more decidedly connected with the extreme of happiness or misery. In such circumstances, trifling is madness. The professed infidel is a reasonable man in comparison with him who admits the Divine inspiration of the gospel, and yet makes it a secondary object of his solicitude.

The Monarch of the Universe has proclaimed a general amnesty of rebellion, whether we give or withhold our belief or our attention; and if an amnesty were all that we needed, our belief or our attention would probably never have been required. Our notions of pardon and punishment are taken from our experience of human laws. We are in the habit of considering punishment and transgression as two distinct and separate things, which have been joined together by authority, and pardon as nothing more than the dissolution of this arbitrary connection. And so it is amongst men; but so it is not in the world of spirits. Sin and punishment there are one thing. Sin is a disease of the mind which necessarily occasions misery; and, therefore, the pardon of sin, unless it be accompanied with some remedy for this disease, cannot relieve from misery.

This remedy, as I have endeavoured to explain, consists in the attractive and sanctifying influence of the Divine character manifested in Jesus Christ. Pardon is preached through him, and those who really believe are healed; for this belief implants in the heart the love of God and the love of man, which is only another name for spiritual health. Carelessness, then, comes to the same thing as a decided infidelity. It matters little in what particular way, or on what particular grounds, we put the gospel from us. If we do put it from us either by inattention or rejection, we lose all the benefits which it is fitted to bestow; whilst, on the other hand, he who does receive it, receives along with it all those benefits, whether his belief has originated from the external evidence, or simply from the conviction of guilt and the desire of pardon, and the discovery that the gospel meets his necessities as a weak and sinful creature,—just as a voyager gains all the advantage of the information contained in his chart, whatever the evidence may have been on which he at first received it.

This last illustration may explain to us why God should have declared *faith* to be the channel of all his mercies to his intelligent creatures. The chart is useless to the voyager unless he believes that it is really a description of the ocean which he has to pass, with all its boundaries and rocks and shoals and currents; and the gospel is useless to man unless he believes it to be a description of the character and will of that Great Being on whom his eternal interests depend. Besides, the nature of the gospel required such a reception in another point of view: it was necessary to its very object that its blessings should be distinctly marked out to be of free and unmerited bounty. When we speak of benefits freely bestowed, we say of them, "You may have them by asking for them,"—distinguishing them by this mode of expression as gifts, from those things for which we must give a price. Precisely the same idea is conveyed by the gospel declaration, "Believe and ye shall be saved." When it is asked, How am I to obtain God's mercy? the gospel answers, that God has already declared himself reconciled through Jesus Christ; so you may have it by believing it. Faith, therefore, according to the gospel scheme, both marks the freeness of God's mercy, and is the channel through which that mercy operates on the character.

It has been my object, throughout this Essay, to draw the attention of the reader to the internal structure of the religion of the Bible,—first, because I am convinced that no man, in the unfettered exercise of his understanding, can fully and cordially acquiesce in its pretensions to Divine inspiration, until he sees in its substance that which accords both with the character of God and with the wants of man; and secondly, because any admission of its Divine original, if unaccompanied with a knowledge of its principles, is absolutely useless.

We generally find that the objections which

are urged by sceptics against the inspiration of the Bible are founded on some apparent improbability in the detached parts of the system. These objections are often repelled by the defenders of Christianity as irrelevant; and the objectors are referred to the unbroken and well-supported line of testimony in confirmation of its miraculous history. This may be a silencing argument, but it will not be a convincing one. The true way of answering such objections, when seriously and honestly made, seems to me to consist in showing the relation which these detached parts bear to the other parts, and then in explaining the harmony and efficiency of the whole system. When a man sees the fulness and beauty of this harmony, he will believe that the system of Christianity is, in truth, the plan of the Divine government, whether it has actually been revealed in a miraculous way or not; and if he finds that the fact of its being inspired really enters into the substance of the system, and is necessary to it, he will be disposed to believe that too.

Let us suppose a man brought from the heart of Africa, perfectly ignorant of the discoveries of Europe, but of excellent parts: let him be fully instructed in all the mathematical and physical knowledge connected with the Newtonian philosophy, but without having the system of astronomy communicated to him; and then let us suppose that his instructor should announce to him that most perfect and most beautiful of human discoveries under the name of a direct revelation from Heaven. The simplicity and the grandeur of the theory would fill his imagination, and fasten his attention; and as he advanced in the more minute consideration of all its bearings, the full and accurate agreement of its principles with all the phenomena of the heavenly bodies would force on his mind a conviction of its truth. He may then be supposed to say to his instructor, "I believe that you have unfolded to me the true system of the material universe, whether you are really under the influence of inspiration or not. Indeed, the most thorough belief in your pretensions could scarce add an iota to my conviction of the truth of your demonstration. I see a consistency in the thing itself which excludes doubting."

We judge of the probability or improbability

of a new idea, by comparing it with those things which we are already acquainted with, and observing how it fits in with them. The complete fitting-in of the astronomical system with facts already observed is the ground of our belief in its truth. The materials of the system lie around us in the appearances of nature; and we are delighted to find an intelligible principle which will connect them all. If a person has paid no attention to these appearances, he will feel proportionally little interest in the discovery of a connecting principle; because he has not felt that uneasiness of mind which is produced by the observation of unexplained facts. A certain degree of education is necessary to excite this uneasy curiosity; and therefore both its pains and its pleasures are confined to a very limited number. But when the facts to be explained are connected with a deep and universal moral interest, and when the most ordinary powers of thinking are equal to the intellectual exertion which is required, there can be no limitation either of the number of the students or of the intensity of the excitement, except in consequence of the most lamentable carelessness.

The materials of the Christian system lie thick about us. They consist in the feelings of our own hearts, in the history of ourselves and of our species, and in the intimations which we have of God from his works and ways, and the judgments and anticipations of conscience. We feel that we are not unconcerned spectators of these things. We are sure that, if there be a principle which can explain and connect them all together, it must be a most important one for us; it must determine our everlasting destiny. It is evident that this master-principle can exist nowhere but in the character of God. He is the universal Ruler, and he rules according to the principles of his own character. The Christian system accordingly consists in a development of the Divine character; and as the object of this development is a practical and moral one, it does not linger longer to gratify a speculative curiosity, but hastens forward to answer that most interesting of all inquiries, "What is the road to permanent happiness?" This question holds the same rank in moral questions, and enters as deeply into the mystery of God's spiritual government, as the corresponding question, "What law regulates and retains a planet in its orbit?" does in the natural world.

If a planet had a soul and a power of choice, and if, by wandering from its bright path, it incurred the same perplexities and difficulties and dangers that man does when he strays from God,—and if the laws which directed its motions were addressed to its mind, and not, as impulses, on its material substance,—its inquiry, after it had left its course, would also be, "How shall I regain my orbit of peace and of glory?" The answer to this question would evidently contain in it the whole philosophy of astronomy, as far as the order of its system was concerned. In like manner, the answer to the inquiry after spiritual and permanent happiness embraces all the principles of the Divine government as far as man is concerned.

The answer to the planet would contain a description of its proper curve: but this is not enough,—the method of regaining it and continuing in it must be also explained. We may suppose it to be thus addressed,—" Keep your eye and your thoughts fixed on that bright luminary, to whose generous influences you owe so many blessings. Your order, your splendour, your fertility, all proceed from your relation to him. When that relation is infringed, these blessings disappear. Your experience tells you this. Retrace, then, your steps, by recalling to your grateful remembrance his rich and liberal kindness. This grateful and dependent affection is the golden chain which binds you to your orbit of peace and of glory."

To man's inquiry after permanent happiness, an answer is given to the same purpose. The path of duty and of happiness is marked out in such precepts as the following: "Thou shalt love the Lord thy God with all thine heart, and soul, and mind, and strength, and thy neighbour as thyself;" "Glorify God in your bodies and your spirits, which are God's;" "Be not conformed to this world, but be ye transformed by the renewing of your minds, that ye may prove what is that good and acceptable and perfect will of God." But this is not enough. Man has wandered from this good path, and in wandering from it he has come under the influence of base attractions, which draw away his will in opposition to the testimony of his conscience, and the acknowledgments of his understanding. To overcome these misleading influences the gospel introduces an attracting principle, most holy in its nature and most constraining in its power. It reveals to him the full danger of his wanderings, but it reveals also to him the full mercy and loveliness of his God. It declares that God so loved the world, as to give his only begotten Son, that whosoever believeth in him should not perish, but have everlasting life— and that Christ hath redeemed us from the condemnation of the law, having endured that condemnation in our stead—and that, on as many as receive him, he confers the privilege of being the sons of God. This is the great truth, for the manifestation and development of which this world was created, and is preserved—and this it is which, when perceived in all its vast reality by the light of the Holy Spirit, transforms the slave of sin into a child of God and an heir of immortal glory. And any one who humbly and candidly considers the Divine character of love and of holiness which is developed in the history of Jesus

Christ will discover in it the true centre of moral gravitation—the Sun of Righteousness set in the heavens to drive darkness and chaos from our spiritual system, and by its sweet and powerful influence to attract the wandering affections of man into an orbit appointed by the will and illumined by the favour of God. According to this system, a grateful and humble affection towards God, founded on a knowledge of his true character, is the principle of order and of happiness in the moral world. The confusion and the restlessness which we see in the world, and which we often experience in our own breasts, give abundant testimony to the truth of this proposition in its negative form. Ignorance and indifference about the character of God generally prevail; we love the creature more than the Creator—the gifts more than the giver—our own inclinations more than his will. The wind is sown, and can we wonder that the whirlwind is reaped? And is it not evident to reason, that an entire conformity to the Ruling Will of the universe is only another name for order and happiness? And can this conformity be produced by any rational being, except by a knowledge and a love of that will? The character of God is manifested in the history of Jesus Christ, for our knowledge and for our love. This manifestation harmonises with the suggestions of reason and conscience on the subject: nay more, it gathers them up, as they lie before the mind in detached fragments; it supplies their deficiencies, and unites them all in one glorious fabric of perfect symmetry and beauty. It meets the heart of man in all its capacities and affections; its appeal is exactly shaped for the elementary principles of our nature. The glorious truth which it reveals is adapted to every mind; it is intelligible to a child, and yet will dilate the understanding of an angel. As the understanding enlarges, this truth still grows upon it, and must for ever grow upon it, because it is the image of the infinite God. Yet, great as it is, it is fitted to produce its effect, wherever it is received, however limited the capacity into which it enters. The principle of the wedge operates as fully at the first stroke as at any subsequent one, although the effect is not so apparent.

I have endeavoured, in the course of these remarks, to give an idea of the mode which seems to me best fitted for illustrating the harmony which subsists between the Christian system and the mass of moral facts which lie without us and within us. I have endeavoured to explain the greatness of its object, and its natural fitness for the accomplishment of that object. He who has not given his earnest attention to these things may call himself an infidel, or a believer, but he has yet to learn what that doctrine is which he rejects or admits.

There is nothing new in this cursory sketch of Christian doctrines. Indeed, I should conceive a proof of novelty on such a subject as tantamount to a proof of error. But I think that the view here taken has not been sufficiently pressed as an argument in favour of the credibility of revelation; for, although an indirect kind of evidence in itself, it seems well fitted for preparing and disposing an unbeliever to examine with candour the more direct proof which arises from historical testimony. And it may also perform the no less important office of infusing into a nominal Christian a doubt as to his sincerity in the profession of a faith which has perhaps neither made a distinct impression on his understanding, nor touched his heart, nor affected his character.

INTRODUCTORY ESSAYS.

INTRODUCTORY ESSAY TO GAMBOLD'S WORKS.

It has long been received as a maxim amongst those who have studied politics, in connection with the philosophy of human nature, that the surest and shortest way of making men good subjects and good citizens is to make them happy subjects and happy citizens. When we say that a man is happy as a subject, or as a citizen, or as a member of any society, we feel that we are just saying, in other words, that he is attached to the government, or state, or society under, or in which he lives; and that he is, of course, disposed to fulfil the duties connected with these relations. It is a maxim founded on the instincts of man; and however it may be neglected in practice, it has too much obvious truth in it to be often controverted in the abstract. Some speculative philanthropists have given this maxim a more splendid and imposing form. They say, "Surround a man with circumstances, and you make of him what you please; command his circumstances, and you command his character." This proposition has not met with so favourable a reception as the other, although it is probably intended to convey precisely the same idea, namely, that a man's character depends on, or is moulded by events and facts external to himself. Indeed, it is impossible to make a man happy in any relation, without commanding his circumstances in some degree, —and so those who admit the first proposition are bound in reason to admit the second. Perhaps the equivocal use of the word *circumstances* may have occasioned some part of the coldness with which it has been received. But, certainly, the chief part is to be ascribed to the unmasked openness with which it comes forward. It assumes a postulate which can never be granted, namely, that it is in the power of man to command circumstances to an indefinite extent. Men may flatter themselves that they can make each other happy in *general*, but when they are brought to *par-*

ticulars, they know and acknowledge that their power is very limited, that they cannot avert pain, or death, or remorse. We are in the habit of calling a man's visible relations, and especially his fortune, health, and family circle, exclusively his circumstances; and as we have many proofs that these circumstances, in their most prosperous state, cannot insure happiness, we think ourselves entitled to deny it of all circumstances. But everything which comes in contact with a man's feeling or thought; everything which occasions joy or sorrow, hope or fear, love or hate, may come properly under the denomination of circumstances. In truth, every feeling arises from some circumstance or cause in contact with us, and yet external to us,—and we know neither happiness nor misery except from circumstances. It is no exaggeration then to say, that *if* we could command the circumstances of a man we could also command his happiness and his character. But of whom can it be said, without exaggeration, that he really can command the circumstances of any sensitive, and intelligent, and immortal being? The relations of human existence are numerous, and to each of these relations belong its peculiar circumstances. Men are fathers, brothers, husbands, sons, friends, masters, servants, rulers, and subjects. They are connected by blood, by business, and by mutual interest—and there are many supposable circumstances in these relations, capable of producing much joy or much sorrow. Who can command these circumstances? Moreover, men are creatures accountable to their Creator. This is the grand and permanent relation. All other relations cease with our life, and even with the lives of others. A man ceases to be a father, when he dies himself, or when all his children are dead,—he ceases to be a husband when his wife is dead,—but he cannot cease to be a creature whilst his existence continues in any mode or form whatever. Who can command the circumstances of this relation? Who is it that can surround the spirit of a man with the light of the Divine countenance? and make this light an abiding and a continual circumstance, accompanying him through life, and bringing into near and distinct vision the undisturbed, unfading, and increasing glories of eternity? Who is he that can remove from a mind convinced of its rebellion against God, and of the justice and awfulness of his displeasure,—who can remove from such a mind the fearful looking for of judgment? Besides, this great relation is not only permanent, it is also the root and the regulator of all the rest. Who placed us in these various passing relations? Our Creator. And our relation to him it is which binds us to fulfil the duties of these relations faithfully.

Of these inferior relations some are more important to our happiness than others. Thus, a man's peace is not so much destroyed by having a worthless servant, or by meeting with a reverse of fortune, as by having a wicked son, or a false friend. Whilst the circumstances belonging to the more important relations of life continue favourable, adverse ones in the less important can be easily supported. But one unfavourable circumstance in the closer and nearer relations will often cast its own dark shadow over a uniform prosperity in all the lower relations. We find that this is the case in the temporary relations of this world, and it is so also in the first and highest relation. A man can generally escape from what is painful in this world's relations. He can leave his country, and whatever it contains, if he does not like it; or, if he cannot do this, he knows that a few years must free him from oppressive rule, from bad health, from unkind friends, and from all other evils peculiar to this life. The thought of a near deliverance is a powerful mitigator of affliction. There are many hours, too, in which he may withdraw himself from his circumstances of sorrow, and then he may have some repose. But if the circumstances of his chief relation, his state before God, be favourable; then, even in the midst of the most overwhelming of this world's calamities, he is an enviable man; there may be, and will be, in spite of occasional eclipses, a deep substantial peace within him, the reflected image of the Sun of Righteousness: he does not look on passing events as the channels of joy or sorrow, but as the indications of his gracious Father's will, calling him to the exercise of faith and love—those holy principles in the perfection of which consists the perfection of happiness: he hath a refuge which the world sees not, and into it he fleeth and is safe: he can even rejoice in tribulations, whilst he thinks of "the man of sorrows," and of the exceeding and eternal weight of glory which is wrought out by these light afflictions which are but for a moment: he looks forward to the glorious morning of the eternal Sabbath, and he feels that he is free and happy for ever.

But if the circumstances of this highest relation be wrong, all is wrong. They may be wrong, and often are, without being felt to be so. There are many who have not set down their relation to God in the list of their relations, who have never regarded his favour or displeasure as circumstances of their condition, and who have never looked into eternity as their own vast, untried dwelling-place, destined to be either their heaven or their hell. And yet this is the chief relation, and these are the chief circumstances of their being. The very root of the moral existence of such persons is dead. Their circumstances are, in truth, most deplorable, and their insensibility to pain from them arises from palsy, not from health. But in some, just so much animation remains that these mighty circumstances are felt to be unfavourable, and then they blacken existence and convert it into anguish. They poison every other relation, and paralyse action in every other duty. Escape is impracticable. The only remedy lies in having these circumstances altered. But who can command these circumstances? Can man command them?

A man who is happy as a father, or a friend, or a citizen, will be found to fulfil the duties of those relations better than another equally conscientious, who is unhappy in these relations; because the one will act cheerfully and from the heart, whilst the other acts from the less lively principle of a sense of propriety. And where there is no conscientiousness on either side, the man who is happy in those relations will fulfil the duties arising out of them naturally, so to speak, whilst the unhappy man will as naturally neglect them. Happiness in one leading relation will often cast its own cheerful glow on the less pleasing circumstances of lower relations, and fill out the concomitant duties with its own life and vigour.

Of what immense moment, then, must it be to have the circumstances of our highest relation, that in which we stand to our Creator, favourable and happy! This would be purifying the fountain, and all the streams would be pure. This would be healing the root, and all the branches would bear good fruit. But we must again return to that most important and critical interrogation, Who can command these circumstances? Who can give a man happiness, in the full view of *all* his relations?

There is nothing absurd in saying, "Command the circumstances of a man, and you command his character;" but there is a strange absurdity in supposing that any power short of omnipotence can command these circumstances; because the chief of our relations is that in which we stand towards Him who is omnipotent. God alone can command these circumstances: no one but God has authority to say that our offences and failures in that relation are forgiven—that a full satisfaction has been made on our behalf to the broken laws of the universal government—that the gates of the family of God are thrown open to us, and that we are invited every moment to speak to him as to a Father, and lean upon him as on an almighty, and faithful, and tender friend—and that the unending duration to which we are advancing is safe and peaceful, full of bliss, and full of glory. The circumstances of that highest relation have been most particularly and fully made known to us in the Bible, that we might have happiness, even the joy of the Lord, which, if really attained by us, will supply strength for the cheerful, and affectionate, and diligent performance of every duty, springing from every relation in life, and will be our comfort and hiding-place in every sorrow.

It has often struck us, as a very remarkable fact, that principles, which are generally recognised as most reasonable and true when applied to the affairs of this life, should be instantly rejected as unreasonable and contemptible when applied to the great concerns of eternity. We can easily suppose the smile of scorn with which a political philosopher would look upon us, if, in reply to his question, "What is the best way of leading back a nation of rebels to obedience to lawful authority, and of engaging them again in the peaceful duties of civil life?" we should return this answer, "Why, the best way is to inculcate upon them the duty of submission, to explain to them the particulars in which that duty consists, and to enforce upon their minds the guilt and the danger of revolt." He would probably give us to understand that we knew nothing about the matter, and he would have very good reason to do so. But is it not strange that, if we asked *him*, "What is the best way of making careless sinful men good subjects of the King of heaven?" he should, almost to a certainty, give us an answer, if he thought the question deserved one at all, in all respects similar to that very reply which he had so deservedly scouted, when made by us to his political problem? He would tell us, "Oh, you must explain their duties to them, and press them on their observance." Suppose, then, that we were just to turn the tables on him, and ask him to answer his own question, and to allow us to answer ours. The answers would be very much alike, except in so far as the revolt against human authority had arisen from misgovernment. He would say, "All unnecessary causes of irritation must be removed, a full and unconditional amnesty must be proclaimed, pledges must be given, which may destroy all possible suspicion of the sincerity of the government, perfect security and safety must be immediately guaranteed, and subsequent promotion in the state ascertained to them, in proportion to their qualifications." We might then say to him, "Take away the first clause of your answer (for there is no unnecessary cause of irritation under God's government), and the remainder may stand for ours. We could particularise, if you wished it, the nature of that amnesty which God has proclaimed, and we could tell of the unutterable pledge of his sincerity, which he has given, even the Son of his love; but your political scheme contains the outline of the Christian dispensation; and your rejection of the latter, whilst you defend and preach the former, ought at least to make you suspect that you are not quite so candid a philosopher as you think yourself, or that, at least, you have made a wrong comparative estimate of the importance of the different relations in which you are placed, having excluded *that one* from the contemplation of your reason which certainly claimed, more than all others, the fulness of its powers." It is most probable, too, that the free and unconditional, and all-including amnesty, which he considers the wisest, and best, and most unassailable position in his political scheme, becomes the marked object of his severe moral censure when it meets him in the Christian plan under the name of free grace. In the real business of life (as he would term it), he fully and intelligently recognises the principle, that the character of a man is moulded by his circumstances; and, therefore, when he designs to affect the character, he turns his skill and his power towards the circumstances which may influence it. He sees plainly within this field, that the true and right fulfilment of the duties belonging to any relation in life is best secured by happiness in that relation. But as soon as his mind is called to another field of contemplation—as soon as eternity is substituted for time, and the Divine authority for this world's rulers, although human beings still continue the subjects to be influenced and operated on—his wisdom seems to forsake him, he rejects measures which, in all analogous cases, he admires, and proposes expedients which he would blush to mention in any other case. There is evidently a most undeniable truth in what the Bible says of the disinclination of the natural man to receive the things of the Spirit. There is nothing astonishing in his rejecting the humiliating fact, that he is deservedly under a sentence of condemnation, which would for ever exclude him from the light and favour of heaven—nor can we wonder that he should hesitate about receiving the fully-developed history of that love which passeth knowledge,—but we may well wonder, that he does not perceive that it is happiness, and happiness derived from known circumstances in this highest relation, as in all other relations, which can alone produce a full and cheerful performance of the duties arising out of it ;—we may well wonder that he, who apprehends so thoroughly the uselessness and inefficiency of mere precepts and delineations of duty in the political, and civil, and social relations of life, when unsupported by circumstances, in those relations, understood and felt as constraining motives of action, should yet exclude from his religious system everything living, and moving, and exciting, all circumstances in the relation of the creature to the Creator, which might lead to happiness, and so animate performance ; whilst he retains only the moral aphorisms and exhortations, which are chiefly intended as the descriptions of the feelings and character which a belief of the revealed circumstances would produce, and which can never, by any process of inculcation, reproduce themselves in minds constructed like ours.

The cheerful and willing obedience which flows from an affectionate heart is the only service acceptable to him whose name is love, and whose law is the law of liberty. And can this be without joy? What draws the affection of the heart? Something amiable, something which pleases, and produces delight. So joy is at the very spring of love and alacrity, and without joy there is nothing graceful, or noble, or free in action.

Do we wish, then, to perform fully the duties belonging to our various relations? Then joy must be infused into the circumstances of those relations. But how is this to be done? Who can command the gifts of fortune or nature? Who can stay the approach of sickness or death? Ay, and what are we to do for the other world? Will the joy of these temporary relations, supposing that we obtain it, carry us forward in healthy and cheerful action through another state of being? Let us be wise in this inquiry, and beware of wasting our time and our strength in vain attempts. Joy infused into the circumstances of any passing relation perishes when that relation perishes. But there is a permanent relation, and it also is the root from which all other relations grow. Oh how desirable to have joy infused *here*, that it might, like living sap, circulate through the whole tree of human relations, and bring forth much fruit on every branch! And praised be our God who hath shed forth joy abundantly on the circumstances of this relation, even joy unutterable and full of glory. He hath drawn aside the veil, and hath let in upon us the light of his own eternal blessedness. He hath done more. He hath said, "Come up hither." He hath changed our scene and our circumstances from earth to heaven—he hath given us a place in the upper sanctuary—he hath surrounded us with the privileges of his children—he hath joined us to the general assembly and church of the first-born, whose names fill the bright and happy rolls of heaven, yea, he hath united us to himself.

But it may be said, "Are the circumstances of this high relation contained in a revelation made to sinners in general, or to certain individuals in particular, for surely there are but few who seem to be happy with God?" The revelation is to sinners in general, but the things contained in it are the circumstances of those only who believe in it. You do not command the circumstances of a blind man when you surround him with visible objects. They are not his circumstances, for they do not come in contact with his thought or feeling. In like manner, the blessings of the gospel are not the circumstances of a man who does not believe the gospel, for they do not come in contact with his thought or feeling. No man can rejoice in that which he does not believe, and it is by peace and joy in believing that the character is purified and sanctified, and made meet for the inheritance of the saints in light.

God has, in his revealed word, surrounded us with circumstances of peace and glory, when we deserved to be surrounded with circumstances of terror and despair. Our hearts have departed from God, and chosen things which he abhors. We think little of him, and feel little about him, and regard not his honour, and desire none of his ways. And yet we are his creatures, and, as such, are bound to obey him at the peril of our happiness for ever. He hath pronounced a sentence of condemnation against every sin—every departure of the will or of the affections from him. Who is there that has not incurred this sentence? And yet, oh! who could bear its infliction? None need bear it but those who refuse the message of mercy: "God so loved the world, that he gave his only-begotten Son, that whosoever believeth in him should not perish, but have everlasting life." The Divine and human natures were united in the person of Christ— he became our representative—he suffered the sentence which had been pronounced against us—Jehovah was well pleased for his righteousness' sake; for thus the law was magnified and made honourable. The work of atonement was declared complete by the resurrection of the Surety; and pardon, and acceptance, and eternal life were proclaimed to be the free gift of God, through the Saviour's name, to the chief of sinners. Joy must be the immediate result of believing that guilt, and danger, and condemnation are done away—that eternity is secure and happy—and that the almighty master of our destiny, the Judge whom we have offended, is our gracious Father, and our kind and compassionate Friend. Hath God then revealed to us circumstances of joy in our eternal relation with himself, and shall we refuse to drink, yea, to drink abundantly of these waters of gladness, that our hearts may be refreshed and filled with a holy alacrity to run in the way of all his commandments? Some who profess to believe the gospel do yet refuse to drink of these waters; because, alas! they have hewn out to themselves, in the passing relations of life, cisterns, which one day they will find to be broken cisterns, that can hold no water.

But some there are, of spiritual minds and humble hearts, who refuse to drink because they think themselves unworthy. "Let the advanced Christian rejoice," say they, "but it would be presumptuous in such polluted sinners as we are to rejoice." Ought not a polluted sinner to rejoice that he is forgiven? and farther, it is this holy grateful joy which God has appointed as the means of cleansing and renewing your nature. "Incline your ear and come unto me," saith the Lord, "hear and your soul shall live: and I will make an everlasting covenant with you, even the sure mercies of David." "Happy are the people that know the joyful sound." If you were called on to rejoice in yourselves, you might wait till you were better, and *long* you would have to wait; but when you are called on to rejoice in Christ, why should you wait? He and his salvation continue always the same, and the greater sinner you are, so much the greater and the more joyful is your deliverance. What made the shepherds rejoice? What made the Ethiopian eunuch and the Philippian jailer rejoice? Nothing in themselves surely; no, it was the exhilarating intelligence that sin was pardoned, that peace was restored between the Holy One who sitteth on the throne of heaven, and the rebellious outcasts of this earth. This is the joy which must lead the way, if we hope to make advances in the Christian course. There is another joy, to be sure, but it never leads the way—it is not called the joy of the Lord, —it consists in the consciousness that the work of God's Spirit is going on in our souls, and that our hearts have, amidst many sins, been faithful to him who loved us. The way to obtain this latter joy is to abound in the former.

We know no author who has illustrated the origin and tendency of the joy of the Lord so simply, so beautifully, or so strikingly as JOHN GAMBOLD. His mind was evidently of a very fine order. In his youth he had mixed philosophical mysticism and theology together. He had formed an elevated, and pure, and holy idea of perfect goodness—he felt his obligation to attain to it—he attempted it long —and at last sunk under the mortifying and heart-chilling conviction that he was only adding sin to sin, without advancing a single step towards his high object. Whilst he was in this melancholy condition, it pleased God that he should meet with one of the Moravian Brethren, who declared to him the simple gospel, "that Christ is made of God unto us wisdom, and justification, and sanctification, and redemption,"—that the only atonement that ever could be made for sin was already made and accepted,—that we neither could take away our guilt by any scheme of our own, nor was it necessary, for Christ's blood had done it,—and that now we are called on and invited, as blood-bought and well-beloved children, to follow him who had so loved us, to keep near to him as the fountain of our life and happiness, and to testify our gratitude to him by obeying his commandments. Pardon is proclaimed through the blood of Christ, and sanctification is the fruit of faith in that pardon. Mr. Gambold gave up his laborious and unsuccessful efforts, and he walked by faith, in humble and peaceful holiness, rejoicing in him who is the strength of his people. The simple child-like joy for sin blotted out did for his soul what all his efforts, and sincere efforts they were, could never accomplish. This joy is his great theme. But we cannot rejoice by *endeavouring* to rejoice, any more than we can love by endeavouring to love. It is by keeping the glorious and blessed circumstances of our relation to God before our mind, that we shall feel, and continue to feel, a natural and unforced joy, which will produce a natural and unforced walk in the way of God's commandments.

But what is the guard against the abuse of this doctrine? Let us look for it in the nature of Christian joy and in its object. Christian joy is not a mere joy for deliverance from misery; it is joy for a deliverance effected by the atonement of Jesus Christ. This joy, therefore, has respect to the procuring cause of the deliverance, as well as to the deliverance itself. In the work of redemption are embodied all the Divine attributes in perfect harmony. Joy becomes thus associated in the mind of the believer with each of these attributes, and it is this same joy which transcribes them on his heart. The object of the gospel, and of the joy arising from a faith in the gospel, is to conform us to the will and likeness of God. The law is thus the guard against the abuse or misinterpretation of the gospel. The law represents the character of God and of perfect happiness; and the gospel was given to associate that character with joy, and thus to write the law upon our hearts. If, then, we believe and rejoice, and yet do not grow in obedience to the law of God, we may be assured that it is not the true gospel which we are believing, nor true Christian joy which we are feeling.

We must turn to the cross, and to the Word which reveals the cross, and to the Spirit who alone can shine upon the Word. Let us not be jealous of joy, but only let us be careful that it is "joy in the Lord." Joy is the first fruit of the gospel of Christ; and if we believe and yet do not rejoice, we may be assured that we have either added to the gospel or taken something from it—it is not the *very* gospel of Christ that we believe. This joy may consist with much sorrow, as it did in the case of those first teachers, who were sorrowful, yet always rejoicing. It takes away the poison from sorrow, and leaves only its tenderness. The exhortation to rejoice in the Lord was not so often repeated without good cause. If this glorious joy once filled our hearts, it would leave no room for sorrow, or for those poor joys which, in their fading, produce sorrow, or for the base, and turbulent, and perplexing anxieties, passions, and appetites which, for the most part, fill up the life of man. If the soul saw itself ever surrounded by the light of that love which shone so bright on Calvary,— if it saw every event and duty in life illuminated by that love,—if the eternal world were ever present to it as its own home, and as the place where redeeming love is the very element of life, where unmixed blessedness reigns, where the tie which unites the Father of spirits to his children is felt in all its ecstatic endearment, and where the whole happy family are continually advancing in their Father's likeness, without fear of change, and without the possibility of falling—O how buoyant would its spirits be! How freely, how boldly, how nobly, and yet how humbly and tenderly would it pass along the course of its existence! In every action it would feel itself a commissioned agent of heaven; it would know that it is called to fulfil purposes which it will require an eternity to unfold; it would have no will of its own, but would act or suffer according to the will of God, looking up to his fatherly face, and rejoicing in his benignant smile.

The mind of Mr. Gambold was evidently deeply affected with these views. The first of the two Sermons which are contained in this volume was preached at a time when the free grace of the gospel was not much known in England; and never did any uninspired Sermon give a plainer or a sweeter exhibition of it. The Drama describes Christianity during the first ages. The author's familiar acquaintance with the Fathers enabled him to put much life and truth into the picture. Did we consider it our business to speak of the merits of this Drama as a poetical work, we could praise it highly. The reader of taste and discernment will discover much in it which proves the very uncommon powers of the author, and which would not have disgraced the first writers in our language. I may instance the last speeches in the dialogue between the two deacons in the opening scene, the exhortations of Ignatius before leaving Antioch, and the whole concluding scene of the Drama. There are, perhaps, other parts which may strike Christians more; as, for example, the scene in which the conversion of the soldier is described, and beautiful most assuredly it is. We remember at present only one passage in Shakespeare which is directly and unequivocally Christian, and that occurs in *Measure for Measure*, in the scene between Isabella and Angelo. She is persuading him to pardon her brother, and she says—

> "All the souls that were, were forfeit once;
> And He that might the vantage best have took
> Found out the remedy: How would you be,
> If He, which is the top of judgment, should
> But judge you as you are? O think on that;
> And mercy then will breathe within your lips,
> Like man new made."

This is certainly in the good, though not in the highest, style of the first genius that probably the world has ever seen, and yet there are many passages in "Ignatius" not inferior to it. There is, to be sure, a degree of stiffness and formality about the piece, but all of that which is disagreeable wears off upon acquaintance, and what remains rather accords with the unworldly character of the persons represented, and so adds to the general truth and interest. His second Sermon, on "Religious Reverence," though not equal throughout, contains some striking thoughts, couched in most powerful phraseology. There is a remarkable expression of devotedness in his first Hymn, and a most sweet and refined loveliness in the poem entitled "The Mystery of Life."

It is impossible to read his works without

being convinced that he enjoyed much communion with God, and was much conversant with heavenly things, and that hence he had imbibed much of the spirit, and caught much of the tone, of the glorified church above. There is a strong reality in his writings; and, oh, it is the great matter after all to have the things of eternity brought into sensible contact with our minds, as present substantial circumstances, producing immediate feeling and action, and not allowed most fatally and foolishly to be mere subjects for conversation, or texts for speculative discussion. If these things be present with us as real circumstances, they will be the sources of real joy, of real confidence for eternity, and of real consistency of conduct whilst we are in this world. Plain unsophisticated minds are the fittest recipients of Christian truth. They have been accustomed to deal with realities, and thus the facts of revelation, when admitted, naturally come to them and operate on them as realities. On the other hand, metaphysicians and poets are very apt to convert the gospel into an ingenious argument and a beautiful dream. We must become as little children, and learn Christianity, not as judges, but as those who are to be judged by it. Let us follow this servant of God as he followed Christ. He was long bewildered in his search after happiness and holiness; at last he found them in the Cross. Leaning on this, he walked in peace and godliness whilst here, and departed hence in the sure hope of glory. His mind was evidently of a high order, his turn of thought is powerful and original, his imagination is of a fine ethereal quality, and his expression vigorous and striking. But our business is not with human genius, it is with Christian doctrine. We do not recommend this book for the passing pleasure which it may afford, but for the permanent profit which, by the divine blessing, may be derived from it. We recommend it as a perspicuous and serious illustration of divine truth; and our prayer is that the eyes of our minds, and of the minds of all who read it, may be opened by the Spirit of God, to discern more and more our need of salvation, and the fulness and preciousness of that salvation which is in Christ Jesus.

"Now unto Him that is able to keep us from falling, and to present us faultless before the presence of his glory with exceeding joy, to the only wise God our Saviour, be glory and majesty, dominion and power, both now and ever. Amen."

T. E.

Edinburgh, *July* 1822.

INTRODUCTORY ESSAY TO BAXTER'S SAINTS' REST.

WE do not arrogate to ourselves so much as to suppose that our commendation can add anything to the authority of such a name as that of RICHARD BAXTER. It is not to commend him, but to render our own series of practical divinity more complete, that we introduce his *Saints' Everlasting Rest* to our readers. He belonged to a class of men whose characters and genius, now universally venerated, seem to have been most peculiarly adapted, by Divine Providence, to the circumstances of their age and country. We do not speak only of those who partook in Baxter's views of ecclesiastical polity; but of those who, under any name, maintained the cause of truth and liberty during the eventful period of the seventeenth century. They were made of the same firm stuff with the Wycliffes, and the Luthers, and the Knoxes, and the Cranmers, and the Latimers of a former age. They formed a distinguished division of the same glorious army of reformation; they encountered similar obstacles, and they were directed, and supported, and animated by the same spirit. They were the true and enlightened crusaders who, with all the zeal and courage which conducted their chivalrous ancestors to the earthly Jerusalem, fought their way to the heavenly city; and rescuing, by their sufferings and by their labours, the key of knowledge from the unworthy hands in which it had long lain rusted and misused, generously left it as a rich inheritance to all coming generations. They speak with the solemn dignity of martyrs. They seem to feel the importance of their theme, and the perpetual presence of Him who is the great subject of it. There are only two things which they seem to consider as realities, the favour of God and the enmity of God; and only two parties in the universe to choose between, the party of God and the party of his adversaries. Hence that heroic and noble tone which marks their lives and their writings. They had chosen their side and they knew that it was worthy of all they could do or suffer for it.

They were born in the midst of conflicts civil and religious; and as they grew up, their ears heard no other sounds than those of defiance and controversy. Thus life was to them, in fact and reality, that warfare which is to many of us only its rhetorical emblem. To this is to be attributed that severity of rebuke and sternness of denunciation, which we are sometimes almost sorry to meet with in their expostulations. But they were obliged to speak loud in order to be heard in those troublous days. They were trained in the language of strife as their mother tongue; and they used that language even in delivering the message of peace. But they did deliver the message of peace, they declared the way of salvation, and they were highly honoured, and invincibly supported by Him who sent them.

The agitated state of surrounding circumstances gave them continual proof of the instability of all things temporal; and inculcated on them the necessity of seeking a happiness which might be independent of external things.

They thus practically learned the vanity and nothingness of life, except in its relation to eternity; and they declared to their fellow-creatures the mysteries of the kingdom of God, with the tone of men who knew that the lightest word which they spoke outweighed in the balance of reason, as well as of the sanctuary, the value of all earth's plans, and politics, and interests. They were upon high and firm ground. They stood in the midst of that tempestuous ocean, secure on the Rock of Ages; and as they uttered to those around them their invitations, or remonstrances, or consolations, they thought not of the tastes but of the necessities of men—they thought only of the difference between being lost and being saved, and they cried aloud, and spared not.

There is no doubt a great variety of thought, and feeling, and expression, to be met with in the theological writers of that class; but deep and solemn seriousness is the common character of them all. They seem to have felt much. Religion was not allowed to remain as an unused theory in their heads; they were forced to live on it as their food, and to have recourse to it as their only strength and comfort. Hence their thoughts are never given as abstract views; they are always deeply impregnated with sentiment. Their style reminds us of the light which streams through the stained and storied windows of an ancient cathedral. It is not light merely, but light modified by the rich hues, and the quaint forms, and the various incidents of the pictured medium through which it passes. So these venerable worthies do not give us merely ideas, but ideas coloured by the deep affections of their own hearts; they do not merely give us truth, but truth in its historical application to the various struggles, and difficulties, and dejections of their strangely chequered lives. This gives a great interest to their writings. They are real men, and not books that we are conversing with. And the peace, and the strength, and the hope which they describe are not the fictions of fancy, but the positive and substantial effects of the knowledge of God on their own minds. They are thus not merely waymarks to direct our journeyings; they seem themselves pilgrims travelling on the same road, and encouraging us to keep pace with them. In their books they seem thus still to journey, still to combat; but oh, let us think of the bright reality!—their contests are past, their labours are over: they have fought the good fight, and they are now at rest, made perfect in Christ Jesus. They are joined to that cloud of witnesses of whom the world was not worthy, and their names are inscribed in the rolls of heaven; yet not for their own glory, but for the glory of him who washed them from their sins in his own blood, and whose strength was made perfect in their weakness.

These were the great men of England, and to them, under God, is England indebted for much of that which is valuable in her public institutions and in the character of her people. They were, indeed, a noble army; they were born from above to be the combatants for truth; they were placed in the gap, and they held their ground, or fell at their posts.

In this army Richard Baxter was a standard-bearer. He laboured much, as well in preaching as in writing; and with an abundant blessing on both. He had all the high mental qualities of his class in perfection. His mind is inexhaustible, and vigorous, and vivacious to an extraordinary degree. He seizes irresistibly on the attention, and carries it along with him; and we assuredly do not know any author who can be compared with him for the power with which he brings his reader directly face to face with death, and judgment, and eternity; and compels him to look upon them, and converse with them. He is himself most deeply serious, and the holy solemnity of his own soul seems to envelop the reader, as with the air of a temple. But on such a subject praise is superfluous, as it is easy; and we shall rather beg the attention of our readers to some observations on his manner of stating Divine truth, and on the interesting subject of the work before us.

In the first place, then, there is perhaps too little appearance of compassion and too much detail in his descriptions of the punishments after death. The general idea is all that is given in Scripture, and even that is rarely insisted on, except by our Lord himself; as if such a fearful denunciation could only have its right effect when pronounced by the lips of him who is love itself. It is not to the statement of the doctrine that we object; but to the manner of doing it. Whatever men may think or feel on the subject, there can be no doubt that the doctrine does stand in Scripture, and assuredly it does not stand there in vain. We must leave the difficulties with God. The light of the last day will dispel all darkness. In the meantime it must be stated; but let it be stated in Scripture language. Let not man use his own words, and far less his own fancy, in describing the future punishments of the impenitent; and above all, let him not speak of them as one at ease; and let him not describe God as taking pleasure in the infliction. There can be no real advantage gained by agitating the imagination on such a subject. Even fear, to be useful, ought to have some calmness in it. And it ought to be remembered that men are not made Christians by terror, but by love. It is the genial ray of the Sun of Righteousness, and not the storm of the Divine wrath, which compels the sinner to lay down the weapons of his rebellion. The steady conviction that misery intolerable must be for ever connected with rejecting the offered mercy of God is the true impression produced by the declarations of the Bible on this matter; and this is a much more efficient and practically useful principle than the terrors of an imagination worked up by a picture of the secrets of that prison-house. Our gracious Master, who suffered in our stead, and whose deep, and solemn, and tender interests in our welfare could not be doubted, did, indeed, in his discourses, always set before men life and death as the solemn alternatives of their choice; but in his mouth it is still the language of affectionate, though urgent persuasion; and he does not lift the veil, except in the parable of the rich man and Lazarus; nor terrify the fancy, nor represent God as taking pleasure in the misery of his creatures. He does not even represent this punishment so much under the form of a positive infliction, as of the natural result of the operation of evil principles on the soul. "*Their* worm dieth not, *their* fire is not quenched." Whose? Their own—the worm and fire within them. Thus also, in other parts of Scripture, the state of the wicked is represented as the reaping of what they had sown, as eating of the fruit of their own way, and being filled with their own devices (Gal. vi. 7, 8; Prov. iii. 31). And in Psalm lxxxi. punishment is described thus, "He gave them up to their own hearts' lusts." The compassion of God for the miseries which sinners bring upon themselves is also often strongly marked by the Bible; for example, in the tears shed by our Lord over the bloody city; in the Divine tenderness exhibited through the whole course of that remarkable history contained in the book of Jonah; and in the duties of a watchman described in Ezekiel xxxiii., "I have no pleasure, saith the Lord, in the death of him that dieth; wherefore turn ye and live." The threatenings of God are all expressions of love. They are the descriptions of the misery of being strangers to God; given for this very purpose, that we may be persuaded to come into his family, and to become fellow-citizens with the saints, and members of the household of faith. God seemed to say in these threatenings, "I cannot bear to lose you, or that you should lose such happiness; behold and see what you are rushing into—a soul at enmity with me must be miserable; come, then, and be my friend and my child." Detailed and prolonged descriptions of future misery seem calculated to injure our view of the Divine character, or to agitate the imagination; or, like violent stimulants to the bodily constitution, to lose their effect, and to deaden the sensibilities to calmer exhibitions of the truth.

But there is another and a more important charge which has been brought against the writings of this great and good man. It is alleged that he does not always mark with sufficient clearness the distinction between the work of God and the work of man, and that he even sometimes gives the idea that we are called on to work out our own pardon, as well as our own salvation or spiritual healing. The close appeals which he so frequently makes to the consciences of his readers may, perhaps, in some degree have given rise to this accusation. A writer who presses so strongly as Baxter does the necessity of a change of heart and character in the Christian needs great caution and accuracy of language in order to avoid expressions which may seem to attribute too much, in the work of salvation, to human effort. Just as a writer, whose great theme is the free grace of the Gospel, would need to be very much on his guard if he would avoid the charge of Antinomianism. The nature of the subject treated on in the book before us may also have assisted in giving this tone to his instructions. He connects pardon and everlasting rest so much together that he sees them and speaks of them as if they were one and the same thing. Now, though in truth they are parts of the same grand plan, yet the one is the commencement, and the other is the consummation of the plan; and the language which is suited to the one is not always suited to the other. Pardon is the starting-point of the Christian course: the saints' rest is the goal. Pardon precedes the race, the saints' rest crowns it. The pardon is universally and freely proclaimed to all without money and without price, without respect to character or condition, as the recompence of the atoning sacrifice of Christ. To this pardon man cannot add, and from it he cannot detract; though he may bar himself from the benefit of it by refusing it admission into his heart. Whereas the saints' rest is entirely dependent on character: it is, in fact, only another name for a character conformed to the will of God. It is, in a sense, the natural reward of diligence in the cultivation of those principles which are implanted by a belief of the pardon. Diligence, therefore, and exertion, ought to be strenuously insisted on in pursuit of the saints' rest; but we must beware of thinking such thoughts or using such language with regard to the pardon. By doing so we shall obscure our views both of the love of God and of the evil of sin. Pardon is the medicine: the saints' rest is the cure accomplished—it is salvation perfected, it is spiritual health. We ought not then to think of labouring for pardon; for it is proclaimed as a thing already past and recorded in heaven; but we ought to labour for the saints' rest, for it is a thing future, and depends on the perfection of principles which are perfected by labour. We ought not to labour for pardon, for it is a medicine already prepared, and freely bestowed, by the great physician of souls; but we ought to labour for spiritual health, in which the saints' rest consists, by continual application to the medicine, and by using the Spirit and the strength which it supplies to support us, amidst the events which befall us, and the duties which we are called to fulfil.

Now, though we are well persuaded that all the parts of Divine truth are so linked together that, if one part is taught to the soul by the

Spirit of God, all the other parts will certainly follow; and that, therefore, a partial obscurity or indistinctness of statement, in the midst of much surrounding light, and perspicuity, and power may not materially impede the progress of a heart towards God; yet we do regret that a greater prominency is not given in Baxter's Works to the doctrine of justification by faith, because the peace of the mind, and the stability of its hopes, and the ardour and confidence of its love, must depend on the degree of fulness with which it can look on God as a Father, who hath forgiven all its iniquities, on a ground altogether independent of its own deservings.

This doctrine is, in truth, the great centre of the Christian system, which gives to all the other parts their symmetry and just proportion. It, in fact, contains all the rest, and we only know them truly when we know them in relation to it. This doctrine it is which constitutes the grand difference between the religion of God and all the religions invented by men. Human systems always place pardon, or the Divine favour, at the end of the race; they would remove condemnation by just making men cease from sinning. Whereas God makes men cease from sinning by first removing the condemnation. This is a stumbling-block to the world and its philosophers. They argue that as sin is the root from which the condemnation sprung, it would be more reasonable to lay the axe to it, than merely to lop the bitter fruit that has sprung from it; and that it is unwise to enfeeble the motives of exertion by giving that in possession which ought to be reserved as the excitement and reward of diligence and obedience.

But the difficulty lies not in the thing itself, but in their ignorance of the signification of the terms employed. They do not know the meaning of sin, or punishment, or obedience, or reward. They consider them merely as external things. If we wish a porter to go a mile for us, we make much surer of his going by promising him half-a-crown on his return than by paying him beforehand. But if we wish to gain the confidence and affection of a man who has prejudices against us, we must begin by substantially proving to him that he may rely on our friendship and services. Now, God desires and requires our confidence and affection. Nothing short of this can satisfy him. It is his great commandment that we should love him with all the faculties of our being; and without this love the most punctual external conformity to his external commandments is a mere mockery and delusion. He is not obeyed by our going the mile, but by our going it out of love to him. He, therefore, begins not merely by holding out to us a future happiness, though he does that too, but by proving himself worthy of all our confidence and all our affection. Obedience, then, consists in active love. And this love can only proceed from a sense of God's excellence and amiableness in general, and of his favour in relation to ourselves. Without this belief in a higher or lower degree, of his favourable regard towards ourselves, there may be a solemn and distant respect, but there can be no filial love, and therefore no full obedience.

We are persuaded that an erroneous view of the object of the ten commandments has misled many as to the nature and extent of religious duty, in this respect particularly. It is true that the ten commandments were given by God's voice from heaven, and it is also true that in the last of them the Legislator claims to himself the sovereignty over the thoughts and intents of the heart, as well as over the act of the hand or the word of the lip; but yet it is no less true that they contain rather a list of prohibitions, and of the most prominent and overt acts of disobedience to the will of God, than a declaration of what that will absolutely is. In human governments, laws are considered as restraints upon natural liberty, and, therefore, everything which is not forbidden by them is permitted. Thus a man may, without being amenable to the law, hate the king as much as he pleases, if he only avoid the commission of any of those acts which are, by statute, construed into high treason. It is certain that the ten commandments are very often interpreted in the same way. They are often supposed to permit that which they do not expressly prohibit. And on this subject we are disposed to think that the error does not so much consist in the misinterpretation of the commandments, as in mistaking the purpose for which they were given, and in supposing that they were ever intended to convey a full and spiritual view of the duty of man to God. For it ought to be remembered that the ten commandments, besides being a religious rule, formed also a part of a code of civil jurisprudence. Jehovah was not only the God of Israel as well as of all the universe, he was also the political King of Israel; and the law of Moses not only gives a view of the Divine character, but also contains the statutes of the state, according to which property was determined, and offences were judged and punished. Religion binds the mind, the law of the land binds the body; God is the only judge of faithfulness or rebellion in the first; man can judge of obedience or disobedience to the second. In the Jewish government these two principles were united —the spirit of religion breathes through the law, and yet the acts prohibited are, with the single exception of the injunctions of the tenth commandment, such as the eye of man could judge of, and such as required to be proved or disproved before their courts by the testimony of human witnesses. This union, however, did not change or materialise the essence of religion. An Israelite who kept the ten commandments to the letter was innocent and righteous in the eye of the law, and of God, considered as the political king of the nation; but he might keep them most strictly to the letter, and yet stand under a heavy charge of guiltiness before God as the spiritual judge of man. This important distinction between the spiritual religion and the material letter of their law appears, however, to have been very generally overlooked by the Jews; they learned to limit their idea of sin to the mere perpetration of the prohibited overt acts of disobedience; they looked to God only as their temporal king, and they became blind to the embracing universality of his claims upon them as their Creator and Spiritual Judge. And the same error is often committed amongst ourselves, without the same apology as the Jews had. There were positive miraculous blessings connected with external obedience under the theocracy, which might naturally lead them to lay great stress on this outside righteousness. And God appeared to them as their national Lawgiver and Judge, requiring this external obedience, and expressing his approbation of it. But the temporal theocracy is no more. God reveals himself in the Gospel solely in his spiritual relation. And when we think of satisfying him by an external obedience, we do him dishonour, and we degrade his law down to a level with our own Acts of Parliament. The offences prohibited in the ten commandments may be considered as the top branches of that tree of revolt which grows naturally in the heart, and brings forth corresponding fruit more or less in the life of every man unrenewed by the Spirit of God. But these branches may be lopped or checked, and yet the strength of the poison may remain undiminished in the root and in the trunk. The true and full law of God is not only directed against this pernicious tree in its root as well as its branches, but it also requires that the soil should be occupied by another plant which may bring forth fruit to the glory of God, "Thou shalt love the Lord thy God with all thy heart, and mind, and soul, and strength." This is the universal and spiritual law of God, and it was given to the Jews, though it does not make a part of their judicial code. It is contained in that solemn and touching recapitulation of mercies, and judgments, and obligations, and duties, which Moses makes to the generation which had been either born or brought up in the wilderness a short time before his own death, and their entrance into the land promised to their fathers. In this address the spirit of the future dispensation breaks forth more distinctly than in that part which was, strictly speaking, their law.

Judaism was throughout a type of Christianity. The wondrous history of the chosen people—their deliverance from Egypt, their wanderings through the desert, their miraculous support during their long pilgrimage, their separation from other nations, their settlement in Canaan, their visible theocracy—were all material emblems of the spiritual kingdom of Christ, and of the spiritual history of the children of God in their journey from this vale of sin and sorrow to the rest prepared for them. Even so their law, in all its parts,—not merely in its ceremonial, but even in its moral precepts,—though it embraced and illustrated the principles of the succeeding dispensation, yet was in itself, to a great degree, literal, and material, and external; and the law of the ten commandments bore to the spiritual law of love a relation somewhat analogous to that which the sacrifices of the tabernacle bore to the perfect atonement of Christ. Those who saw in the sacrifices no more than a ceremonial purification from external pollutions, or a mode of deliverance from external evils, would see no more in the ten commandments than a rule of external obedience. Whilst those who saw under that veil of rites a manifestation of the combined mercy and holiness which constitute the spiritual character of God in relation to sinners—those who saw under it the type of that great atonement, on the ground of which the Divine justice is even glorified in the pardon of the offenders, such Israelites would also discover the spiritual law of love under the ten commandments, and would feel their hearts drawn to its observance. And in like manner, those who had found out that heart-love was the obedience which God required would not rest satisfied until they had also discovered the true meaning of the sacrifices. They would feel assured that the same principle in the mind of God which prompted him to demand the hearts of his creatures would prompt him also to make such a discovery of his own character as would draw their hearts, and make obedience easy and delightful. They would look for something else than mere authority to enforce such a command; and they would find it in the spiritual antitype of all these ceremonies. Christ came not to destroy the law and the prophets, but to fill them out. They were but sketches and cartoons. He came to fill up their shadowy outlines with all the substance of real action, and all the rich colouring of spiritual affections. The ten commandments, taking into account the Christian modification of the fourth, are as binding now as ever they were, because the duties contained in them spring out of the eternal relation between God and man; but the most exact adherence to their letter will not defend us from the charge of spiritual delinquency before the Searcher of hearts.

When the law of God comes to a man only in the shape of prohibitions, he is apt to consider it as a hard and severe thing, and to count his own uneasy submission to it an act of price and merit. He has unwillingly abstained from some indulgence, and he lays up this price of self-denial in his treasury, as something on which he may afterwards found a hope or a claim before God. But when the law makes a demand upon our heart, the matter is changed entirely. In the first place, it is evident that he who makes the demand is himself full of affection towards us, for what but love could make him desire possession of our hearts? and, in the next place, the idea of merit is altogether thrown out, because who is it that can say that he has loved with all his heart? and besides, the very thought of forming to ourselves a claim destroys the fulness of the obedience, as it taints the freedom and generosity of love.

A prohibitory law allows a man to think that he has fulfilled duty, and even that he has done certain things beyond the requirements of duty; or, in other words, supererogatory. But the law of love sets duty, like the horizon, always before us, at the utmost extent of vision; for love urges to do all that we can do, and then thinks all too little.

If the law of God could be truly obeyed by mere self-denial and exertion, then pardon, or the expression of divine favour, might properly have been reserved, and held out as the ultimate reward of diligence. But if the heart is positively required, and if love be the obedience demanded, as well as the heaven promised by the Bible, then we must have something to enforce it more cogent than either a command or the expectation of a reward. And this we have in the gift of Christ, which is both the pledge of pardon and the proof of love.

It may appear to some that the argument which has been stated is not of much importance in these Christian days, as they are called. But the error which it combats is not confined to any country or to any age. Men still desire to change the spiritual, heart-searching God, into a temporal king, who judges only by the outward act, and who is satisfied with pious forms and social integrity. It is this error which has to a great degree unchristianised even the form and profession of the Church of Rome, and which, more or less, unchristianises the religion of Protestants. We may call it Judaism, or we may call it Popery, but it is the error of the human heart, more openly professed indeed by some than others, but prevalent universally under various shapes and names, until rooted out by the Spirit of the living God.

It is the knowledge of duty which gives us the knowledge of sin. And a knowledge of the true nature of these two things makes the

Gospel absolutely necessary to the heart. Sin is the transgression of the first and great commandment—it is a departure of the heart from God. And why does the heart depart from God? Is he not good; is he not gracious; is he not worthy of our highest love, and gratitude, and confidence? Yes, no one denies this. How then does it come to pass that the heart departs from God? The explanation is, that our affections are bound to God only whilst the view of his love and his excellency is present to the mind. Had the tempter dared to assail Adam whilst he was walking with God in the garden and drinking in life and light from his communion with him, can we doubt what the result would have been? God is light, and walks in light—a light pure and unapproachable by evil; and when Adam walked with him he also was surrounded by that light, and was defended by it as by a shield. It is in the absence of the sun that the glow-worm and the ignis-fatuus are seen; and it is in the absence of the light of the Divine presence that the things of sense and of time assume a false splendour, and, like the wandering fires of nature, lure men to destruction. He who walketh in the day stumbleth not, for he hath the light of this world; he sees things as they are; he is not exposed to the delusion of false appearances; he can distinguish between the beaten road and the morass; he walks confidently and safely, for it is light which leads him. It is the property of light to make manifest; and the more elevated the kind and the degree of the light is, the greater will be the perfection and the truth of the manifestation. What then must the perfection and truth of that manifestation be, which is made by the spiritual presence of the Father of lights; and how great must be the security and confidence of those who walk in it!

In this light Adam walked during the happy days of innocence. And whilst he thus looked on the excellence and the beauty of God, he was irresistibly attracted to him, and he could not sin, for the law of love was written on his heart.

The presence of God was thus the source and the security as well as the reward of his continued love and obedience. But he went out from the presence of God—he ceased to contemplate God—and the light of the Divine perfections faded from his spiritual vision. In this season of absence or forgetfulness love abated (for love lives by contemplating what is excellent), the tempter came, and Adam fell. Ah! wherefore did he leave that blessed light which was a glory and a defence—which would have scared away the powers of darkness, and guided his steps, and kept him from falling? Verily, it is an evil and bitter thing to depart from God. What was his condition now? Alas, how changed! Instead of walking with God as a friend, he dreaded and shunned him as an enemy. His backslidings reproved him, and his own conscience became the dreadful executioner of that sentence which excluded him from the family and favour of God. As he had refused to walk in the light, he was shut out from the light—he had chosen a lie, and he received it for his portion—he had disregarded the smile of Jehovah, and now he could think only of his frown.

Thus not only did sin become its own punishment, but this punishment became a fruitful source of further sin. It was the contemplation of the excellency, and a sense of the paternal favour of God, which produced and expanded the principles of holy love and obedience in the heart of Adam. The cessation of this contemplation, and the forgetfulness of this paternal favour, were the very causes of his fall; and now these causes are fixed upon him—they become the very circumstances of his existence. He cannot contemplate God, for he feels himself banished from his presence —he cannot enjoy the sense of his paternal favour, for condemnation has been pronounced against him.

Adam's perfection had flowed from, and consisted in this,—that his affections were powerfully and permanently attracted by the contemplation of the holy love and kindness of God. When this attraction ceased, his perfection ceased. What then must the consequence have been when the Divine love and favour were changed into displeasure? Evidently repulsion instead of attraction. It is the smile, and not the frown—it is the favour, and not the condemnation of God, which shows forth love; but it is only his frown and his condemnation which the convicted and unpardoned rebel contemplates: and thus the estrangement of his heart becomes more and more confirmed—darkness is his guide, and it leads him to thoughts and deeds of darkness. These thoughts and deeds, he feels, call for a further condemnation; and the fear of this removes him still farther from God. There is no limit to this tremendous series but in the riches of Divine grace. Perhaps the most overwhelming circumstance in the miserable condition supposed is, that even the remaining good of the heart opposes our return to God. All our remaining sense of the excellency of holiness, and all the loathing and condemnation of our own pollution, which we may yet feel, makes us shun the Divine presence. The knowledge and approbation of what is right, without some view of forgiving love, can do little more, in the heart of a weak and sinful creature, than record and repeat the sentence of condemnation against itself,—and teach it, that any misery is to be preferred to that of looking in the face of an offended God.

Is there not then a true philosophy in that system which would make men cease from sinning by removing the condemnation of sin? Is there not a true wisdom in that religion which would draw men from works of darkness, by surrounding them again with heavenly light? And is there not a Divine glory in that plan which would overcome evil by good—which would annihilate distance by annihilating fear—and which would expel enmity from the soul by satisfying it with the abundance of grace?

The perfection of a creature does not consist in its own self-possessed powers, but in the maintenance of its proper place in relation to its Creator; and the name of that place is Constant Dependence. This place can be held only by affectionate confidence; and this requires a constant sense of the favourable presence and protection of God. Men sometimes puzzle themselves by contrasting the moral strength attributed to Adam with the facility of his fall. But Adam's strength is only another name for his love to God; and that love depended entirely on the view which he took of His character in general, and of His relation to himself in particular. Whilst he viewed Him as his omnipresent and ever-gracious Friend, he loved Him; or, in other words, he was strong. When he lost this view, from any cause, there would be a proportional diminution of his strength. And after his offence, when he viewed Him as his condemning Judge, his love would be changed into fear and estrangement; that is to say, his strength would become weakness.

It must be so—it cannot be otherwise, in the nature of things. Love is the obedience of the heart; and that is the obedience which God requires. And this love, in the heart of a hitherto sinless creature, can only proceed from, or be maintained by a sense, and a continued sense, of the holy complacency of God; and, in the heart of a sinful creature, by a sense, and a continued sense, of the holy compassion of God. This going forth of the heart and the thought towards God is to the spiritual man what his locks were to the unshaven champion of Israel. It is the channel through which the omnipotent God communicates himself to his children. Whilst this channel continues unbroken and uninterrupted all is safe, but when a created thing is permitted to interpose itself between the soul and the face of God, the charm is broken—the divine current ceases to flow in—he who before was strong becomes weak—and those Philistines who had often fled before him now put out his eyes, and make him grind in their prison.

"Abide in me," says the Head of the redeemed family, "and I will abide in you." Thus shall ye bring forth much fruit; and thus shall ye "ask what ye will, and it shall be done unto you." To this object, therefore, ought Christian effort mainly to be directed; for here the Christian's strength lies, and here only. Here only he finds an object which will satisfy and sanctify every faculty of his being. His moral sense, his affections, and his desire of happiness are here filled and captivated. How different this from the effort of the world's morality! The world's morality, even in its highest strain, is mere self-denial, and a painful struggle against nature. It is, however, a noble struggle. And, assuredly, when we look at those who, unaided by the light of revelation, have trod this uphill path; and who, by the strong effort of an upright will, have quelled the passions and feelings which rebel against truth and reason, we cannot but admire them; and little do we envy those who can refuse them this tribute. But though it is a noble spectacle, it is yet a melancholy one. It is an unequal warfare. The citadel is betrayed; the heart is in the hands of the enemy. The conqueror is unhappy, even in his victory; for what has he achieved? He has not really overcome his antagonists; he has only prevented their eruption. He has imprisoned them in their own favourite residence—his inmost heart, where they feed on his very vitals. On the Christian system the cure begins at the heart; and the moral progress is a healthy progress of the whole man, and not a temporary submission of one part of the mind to another.

There is no self-denial in the character of God; it is his delight to do that which is good. Neither would there be any self-denial in our virtue if we perfectly loved God; because that love would find its highest gratification in a conformity to the will of God. But how are we to grow in this love? How is our holiness to be purged from self-denial? No otherwise than by abiding in the view of God, as revealed in Jesus Christ. This rule differs only in words from the apostolic precept, "Pray without ceasing." It embraces the whole armour of

God, and gives peace as well as security. The heart must be directed towards God, the Father of mercies; and then, even in this prison, although we may still feel our fetters, our locks will begin to grow like Samson's; and, however we may groan under the burden of life and remaining corruption, yet shall we, like him, also triumph at our death, and be made more than conquerors, through him that loved us.

For it is not till after death that we are to expect unmixed happiness. Our moralists need not be apprehensive that Christianity, by the greatness of its present gifts, extinguishes hope for the future. There is something kept in reserve to animate exertion and to reward perseverance. The gospel does not expend all its treasures in this life. Great indeed, and unspeakable, are the blessings which it bestows even here; but they are not given without alloy—they serve but as foretastes to excite our longings for the joy set before us. The gospel teaches us to deny ungodliness and worldly lusts. And it teaches this only by directing our thoughts, not only *back* to the cross and to the pardon which was there sealed; and *around* us, to that mercy which continually embraceth those who trust in the cross; but also *forward*, to the blessed hope of the Saviour's appearing, and to the rest which remaineth for the people of God. Yes, every sin is full of sorrow; and every day on earth is full of sin. Man also "is born to trouble, as the sparks fly upward." And although the believer does feed on angels' food, and although the blessed Spirit does comfort his heart by the disclosures of that love which passeth understanding, yet is he often made to feel the length of the way and the barrenness of the land. And often does his evil heart of unbelief grieve that Comforter, and tempt him to depart. He feels that he daily wounds the love that bled for him; and that is bitter, even in the midst of forgiveness. He also sees God dishonoured, and his law trampled on by his fellow-creatures. And thus he is taught that this is not his rest; and that he hath no abiding city here. These things made the Psalmist say, "Oh that I had wings like a dove, for then would I fly away and be at rest,"—they drew from Jeremiah that plaintive cry, "Oh that I had, in the wilderness, a lodging-place of wayfaring men; that I might leave my people and go from them,"—and they even forced Elijah, a man destined to enter heaven by another gate than that of death, to request for himself that he might die. Now all these men had much enjoyment of God in this world, as we read in other parts of their history; but the vast disproportion between their enjoyment of him here, and their expected enjoyment of him in the other world, made them, as well as the saints under a clearer dispensation, feel and confess that presence in the body is absence from the Lord.

And yet future glory is not desired by a Christian as an entirely new and hitherto unknown thing, but as the full accomplishment of a blessedness already begun, though too much impeded here by corruption within and sorrow without. Christianity was not an entirely new thing to pious Jews; but yet its light so far excelled that of their introductory dispensation as to make it appear but darkness in the comparison. They saw it afar off, but the prospect was so dim that Isaiah calls it, "that which eye had not seen, nor ear heard, nor the heart of man conceived." Even so we may say of Christian joy, as we must confess of Christian character in this life, that it hath no glory, by reason of the glory that excelleth. We can place no limits to that future glory, but in the will of Him whose goodness and power are equally unlimited.

That family which God hath adopted in Christ Jesus, for their spiritual good, he hath subjected in this world, as he did the Captain of their salvation, to affliction. They are, however, supported under it by the assurance that, as they are joint-heirs with Christ in suffering, they shall be so also with him in glory. The anticipation of that glory is a characteristic feature of the family. Whilst they remain on earth, their eyes are fixed on it, and their earnest expectation waiteth for its perfect development in the full manifestation of their privileges as the sons of God. As the gospel was the same *in kind*, from the first promise of the woman's seed in Eden until the day of Christ's ascension from Mount Olivet, and only varied in the degree and clearness of its revelation; so also the character and joy formed upon it and by it, must be the same in kind for ever, and will only vary in the degree of its development. This accounts for the same name being sometimes given to different stages in the process. Thus, in one place we are told that believers have already received the charter of adoption in that revelation which addresses them as children, and authorises them to speak of God as their Father. And, at the distance of a few verses, these same believers are described as waiting for the adoption, namely, the redemption of their body. The resurrection is here called the adoption, because it is the concluding step in the process of adoption; it is that act of omnipotent mercy by which the last trace of condemnation shall be obliterated—by which this mortal shall be clothed with immortality, and this corruptible with incorruption. There is but one joy, and one adoption; but they contain the principle of infinite expansion and enlargement. The light of revelation enables us to trace their progress till the morning of the resurrection, when the risen saints shall sit down with Christ upon his throne; and there it leaves them, hid in the future eternity.

Then their joy shall be full—they shall ever be with the Lord—they shall be made pillars in his temple, and go no more out. But still the principle of progress will be in action. The joy which fills them will expand their capacity of enjoyment; and their increasing capacity will be filled with an increasing joy. Their joy will increase because their powers and capacities of comprehending and loving God will increase; but still the great object itself, the source of all their joy, remains eternally the same—the character of God, revealed in Christ Jesus.

It is sweet to look forward to the restitution of all things—to think of a world where God is entirely glorified, and entirely loved, and entirely obeyed—where sin and sorrow are no more—where severed friends shall meet, never again to part—where the body shall not weigh down the spirit, but shall be its fit medium of communication with all the glorious inhabitants and scenery of heaven—where no discordant tones or jarring feelings shall interrupt or mar the harmony of that universal song, which shall burst from every heart and every tongue to Him who sitteth upon the throne, and to the Lamb. And it is not only sweet, but most profitable to meditate on these prospects. It is a most healthful exercise. It brings the soul into contact with that society to which it properly belongs, and for which it was created.

The world thinks that these heavenly musings must disqualify the mind for present exertion. But this is a mistake, arising from an ignorance of the nature of heaven. The happiness of heaven consists in the perfection of those principles which lead to the discharge of duty; and therefore, the contemplation of it must increase our sense of the importance of duty. That happiness, as has been already observed, is not entirely a future thing; but rather the completion of a present process, in which every duty bears an important part. The character and the happiness of heaven, like the light and heat of the sunbeams, are so connected, that it is impossible to separate them; and the natural and instinctive desire of the one is thus necessarily linked to the desire of the other. Full of peace as the prospect of heaven is, there is no indolent relinquishment of duty connected with the contemplation of it: for heaven is full of action. Its repose is like the repose of nature—the repose of planets in their orbits. It is a rest from all controversy with God—from all opposition to his will. His servants serve Him. Farewell, vain world! no rest hast thou to offer which can compare with this. The night is far spent; soon will *that* day dawn, and the shadows flee away.

The Saints' Everlasting Rest was written on a bed of sickness. It contains those thoughts and feelings which occupied, and fortified, and animated the author as he stood on the brink of eternity. The examples of heavenly meditation which he gives really breathe of heaven; and the importance of such meditation, as a duty, and as a mean of spiritual growth, is admirably set forth, and most powerfully enforced. And is it not a most pernicious madness and stupidity to neglect this duty? Is it not strange that such prospects should excite so little interest? Is it not strange that the uncertainty of the duration of life and the certainty of its sorrows, do not compel men to seek refuge in that "inheritance which is incorruptible, undefiled, and which fadeth not away"? Is it not strange that the offers of friendship and intimate relationship which God is continually holding out to us, should be slighted, even in competition with the society of those whom we cannot but despise and reprobate? Is it not strange that we should, day after day, allow ourselves to be duped by the same false promises of happiness which have disappointed us just as often as they have been trusted? Oh! let us be persuaded that there is no rest in created things. No: there is no rest, except in Him who made us. Who is the man that can say he has found rest elsewhere? No man says it. May God open our hearts as well as our understandings to see the truth, that we may practically know the insufficiency, and hollowness, and insecurity of all earthly hopes; and that we may be led, in simplicity and earnestness, to seek, and so to find our rest in Himself.

T. E.

EDINBURGH, *February* 1824.

INTRODUCTORY ESSAY TO RUTHERFORD'S LETTERS.

To understand the doctrines of the Bible aright, it is of the greatest importance to form just ideas of what is meant by the word "salvation," as many of the practical errors into which men have fallen on the subject of Christianity have arisen from a misconception of this term: some supposing it to refer merely to the pardon of sin, and others to an undefined happiness in a future state.

To assist our inquiries into this most interesting subject, it is of importance to examine the different passages of Scripture in which this term is used, and to compare it with other terms which are frequently employed as synonymous with it.

In Scripture the term *salvation*, with its grammatical branches, is applied to the bodies as well as to the souls of men. When applied to the body, it varies in its meaning according to the state or condition of those who are the subjects of it. These conditions are chiefly two, namely, first, a state of danger arising from causes external to the body, such as shipwreck, war, or famine; and, secondly, a state of danger arising from disease within the body.

First, When the term *salvation* is applied to persons in a state of danger from external causes, it means an external act, corresponding to the nature of the danger by which the cause of the danger is removed, and security restored. Thus, in the description of the shipwreck, given in the 27th chapter of the Acts, the word σώζω is used to signify deliverance from the danger of the sea: "And when neither sun nor stars in many days appeared, and no small tempest lay on us, all hope that we should be saved was then taken away."—"Paul said to the centurion and to the soldiers, Except these abide in the ship, ye cannot be saved." And in the following chapter, verse 1st, the word translated *escaped* is derived from the same root. In the Septuagint the same word is applied to those who have escaped from battle.

When our Lord, in the agony of his soul, prays that the bitter cup of suffering might pass from him, he uses the same word: "Now is my soul troubled; and what shall I say? Father, save me from this hour: but for this cause came I unto this hour." Jude applies it to the deliverance from the land of Egypt: "I will therefore put you in remembrance, though ye once knew this, how that the Lord, having saved the people out of the land of Egypt, afterward destroyed them that believed not." In these cases salvation means simply such a change upon the external circumstances, in which the body is placed, that danger is removed, and safety recovered. No change is produced on the body itself, but only on its situation, with regard to other things.

Secondly, When this term is applied to the case of persons labouring under disease, it signifies an internal operation, suited also to the evil which it remedies, by which the inward principle of the malady is counteracted, and the bodily organs restored to healthful exercise. This is the most common use of the word in the New Testament, when it refers to the body. In this sense it occurs in most of the narratives of our Lord's miraculous cures, and is rendered in our translation by various English phrases, such as "made whole"—"For she said within herself, If I may but touch his garment, I shall be whole. But Jesus turned him about; and when he saw her, he said, Daughter, be of good comfort; thy faith hath made thee whole. And the woman was made whole from that hour. And whithersoever he entered, into villages, or cities, or country, they laid the sick in the streets, and besought him that they might touch if it were but the border of his garment: and as many as touched him were made whole."——"Healed"—"They also which saw it told them by what means he that was possessed of the devils was healed." ——"He shall do well"—"Then said his disciples, Lord, if he sleep, he shall do well." In these cases salvation does not mean a change upon circumstances external to the body, but upon the internal condition of the body itself.

The distinction between these two classes of cases is obvious. In both an external agent is supposed to apply the remedy, but the operation of this agent differs according to the nature of the evil. In the first class it is directed to the external circumstances in which the body is placed—in the second it is directed to the body itself.

We frequently see these two kinds of salvation conjoined—thus a man is imprisoned on suspicion of a crime, and in consequence of the unhealthiness of the place is seized with the jail fever—at last he is acquitted, and his liberation is followed by restored health. Here the one salvation is the effect of the other, and is indeed the only thing which could make the other valuable. Take another instance: A man loses his health from the use of improper food—a benevolent person, by supplying him with proper food, restores his health. Here the external evil is unwholesome food, and the internal is disease. There are also two kinds of salvation, corresponding to these two evils, the one of which, however, is entirely subservient to the other. The change of food is made simply for the purpose of restoring health, and if this effect does not follow, nothing has been accomplished which can properly be called salvation, the whole plan has failed. Salvation then properly refers to the ultimate object in the series. If a man is simply in danger of being lost by shipwreck, his ultimate object is to be safe on dry land; but if the fear of this danger has deprived him of his reason, then the recovery of his mental health becomes the ultimate object, and the salvation from shipwreck becomes merely a step to the salvation of his reason. So if a man has the disease of cancer, he may be delivered from the cancer by the knife; but then the salvation from the cancer is subservient to the salvation of his health, and unless this consequence follows, the object has failed.

The minuteness of these observations may seem tedious, but we have been led to them from the persuasion, that a greater attention to the analogy which subsists between the treatment of the body under danger or disease, and the gospel scheme of salvation, would very much increase the accuracy of our ideas on religious subjects. Salvation from bodily disease is frequently expressed by the word "life:" "Jesus saith unto him, Go thy way; thy son liveth. And the man believed the word that Jesus had spoken unto him, and he went his way."—"And he besought him greatly, saying, My little daughter lieth at the point of death: I pray thee, come and lay thy hands on her, that she may be healed; and she shall live." In which last instance, "she shall live" is used as explanatory of "that she may be healed." Life in these cases evidently signifies the full exercise of the animal faculties, and when it follows sickness, is synonymous with a confirmed cure. This same salvation is also expressed by the term "loosing," or freeing from the bondage of pain: "And ought not this woman, being a daughter of Abraham, whom Satan hath bound, lo, these eighteen years, be loosed from this bond on the Sabbath-day?"

We now proceed to consider the import of the term salvation when applied to the soul. Salvation, when applied to the soul, refers also to two kinds of evils which, though different in their nature, are yet always conjoined—the one being external to the soul, the other internal—the first consisting in the sentence of God against the soul, on account of disobedience, the second consisting in the diseased and depraved state of the soul itself.

The first of these evils, namely, the sentence of God against the soul on account of disobedience, consists in an eternal exclusion from the family and favour of God. The second evil, namely, the diseased state of the soul itself, consists in that disposition which leads to disobedience. Salvation from the first of these evils may be termed a judicial acquittal. Salvation from the second, a recovery of spiritual health.

In order to understand and adore the wisdom of God in redemption, it is necessary to understand the way in which these two kinds of salvation are connected, for they are never disjoined. Now there are two ways in which things may be conjoined, namely, by arbitrary connection and by natural connection. As an instance of the first, we may take the obligation under which a man lies to take certain oaths, when he is intrusted with certain offices under Government. There is no natural or necessary connection between these two things, the connection arises out of law or usage : the man *may* take the oaths without getting the office. As instances of the second, we may take the connection which subsists between a man's being a father and having a kindness for his children, or between a man's receiving a favour and feeling gratitude.

It may here be argued, with justice, that as God is the God of nature, every connection which he appoints becomes a natural connection. This is not denied, and all that is meant here by natural connection is such a relation between two things, that to our minds the existence of the one appears indispensable to the existence of the other, or at least that the existence of the one appears to us, in the ordinary course of things, to lead to the existence of the other.

Let us now take a short view of the gospel system, that we may perceive *how* the two kinds of salvation therein revealed are connected, that is, how pardon through a Saviour is connected with the recovery of spiritual health, and also that we may perceive which of the two is the *ultimate object* in God's dealings with men.

The Bible informs us that man has fallen from God's favour, and from his own natural happiness, by having a will different from God's will, and by acquiring a character and pursuing a conduct opposite to God's character and conduct. Mere pardon to a creature in this situation would be comparatively of small consequence, because his unhappiness arose necessarily out of his character, and, therefore, unless his character were changed, his unhappiness remained the same. The enjoyments of God's family were things contrary to his corrupted taste and choice, and, therefore, his free admission into them could be no blessing to him. In order to his happiness, the restoration of his lost privileges must be accompanied by a restoration of the capacity to enjoy them. For this reason, when God invited his rebellious creatures to return to his favour and family, he did it in such a way that the soul which truly accepted of the invitation imbibed at the same time the principles of a new character.

There is a difference between the body and the mind which should here be taken notice of. The body may be perfectly capable of enjoyment, and yet at the same time perfectly miserable, in consequence of being precluded from the means of enjoyment. Thus a man in a perfect state of health may be made unhappy by being fettered in a noisome dungeon, where he is debarred from the exercise of those animal faculties, the gratification of which constitutes animal enjoyment. But we cannot apply this reasoning to the mind. A perfectly healthful state of mind, according to the appointment of him who changeth not, is inseparably connected with mental enjoyment. The happiness of God arises necessarily out of his character, and the mental health of intelligent creatures, which is in fact nothing more nor less than a resemblance to the character of God, must also be inseparably connected with happiness. So that perfect mental health is not simply the *capacity* for enjoyment; it may perhaps more properly be said to constitute enjoyment itself. The same, or similar causes, must produce the same or similar effects, and if the character of God is the cause of his happiness, a similar character (with reverence be it spoken) must produce a similar happiness. And this happiness can be produced by no other character, for that would be to suppose that opposite causes could produce the same effects.

If this be so, it follows, that a restoration to spiritual health, or conformity to the Divine character, is the *ultimate object* of God in his dealings with the children of men. Whatever else God hath done with regard to men has been subsidiary, and with a view to this; even the unspeakable work of Christ, and pardon freely offered through his cross, have been but means to a further end; and that end is, that the adopted children of the family of God might be conformed to the likeness of their elder brother—that they might resemble him in character, and thus enter into his joy. This is spiritual health, and it is acquired by the blessing of God upon the reception and faithful use of the means which he hath appointed and made known to us in the history of his mercy through a Saviour. A free offer of pardon through the Son of God is termed *salvation*, just in the same way that a medicine is, in common language, called *a cure;* that is, they do not strictly constitute salvation—they only produce it. Before entering on the consideration of those passages which confirm this view of the subject, we shall endeavour to make our meaning more distinctly understood. It must be remembered always, that the love of God with the whole heart is not only the sum of all that duty which is positively enjoined on us by the

Divine law, under an awful penalty, but also, that it is the only principle which can produce or maintain spiritual health. Our failure, therefore, in obedience to this law of love, not only exposes us to the penalty denounced against disobedience, but also plants in our souls the seeds of disease.

Let us suppose that the inhabitants of any district were liable to an epidemic disorder, which, from the partial derangement accompanying it, naturally unfitted its victims for the exercise of civil rights; and that there were, in the neighbourhood, certain salubrious springs which had the virtue of counteracting the tendency to disease in those who used them, the waters of which were very palatable to those who were in health, but very disagreeable to those who were infected. Let us suppose, further, that the Government, anxious for the well-being of the people, should enact a law, binding every individual to drink these waters at fixed periods, under the penalty of forfeiting all civil rights and immunities, in case of disobedience; thus adding the sanction of law to the constitution of nature. In these circumstances, it is evident that disobedience would be attended by two distinct consequences: first, by disqualification for holding any office in the state, as the legal penalty of disobedience; and, secondly, by a disease (from not using the antidote) which would, of itself, naturally unfit the subject of it from holding any office, even were he not excluded by law, and which would also oppose its own cure, by producing a strong repugnance to the only medicine which could remove it. Their natural repugnance to the waters would also be strengthened by irritation against the Government under whose condemnation they lay, and by the persuasion that obedience could now be of no use, because the penalty was already incurred.

In this supposed case, we see obedience, health, and the enjoyment of civil privileges united both by law and nature on the one side; and disobedience, civil disqualifications, and disease, as closely united on the other. We see also that this disease can only be removed by a return to obedience, and that this obedience can only be produced by some motive powerful enough to overcome the distaste for the remedy. As health, and the enjoyment of civil privileges, were, from the outset, inseparably connected in the mind of the Government, and as the law was made simply for the purpose of giving an additional motive for using the necessary means of preserving health, so, if the malady should become generally prevalent (the original connection between health and civil privileges still subsisting, and being itself the real ground of the present disqualifications), the views of Government would become primarily directed to those means by which the people might be induced to return to the use of that remedy which could alone restore health, and fit them for the exercise of those privileges for which they had disqualified themselves both by law and nature. The reason of this is obvious, because the removal of the legal disqualifications could be of no possible use whilst the disease continued, except in so far as it acted as a motive with the diseased outlaws for applying the remedy, both by showing them that the road to preferment was now set open, if they were only fit for it, and also by manifesting the kindly disposition of Government, and thus exciting them to gratitude and obedience.

Although it is perhaps impossible to make out a perfect analogy between the things of the visible and invisible worlds, yet there appear to us to be some circumstances, in this case, which bear very much on the relation which, according to the Bible, subsists between God and man.

The rights and immunities of God's family consist in possessing the favour of God, in approaching to him at all times as our Father, in enjoying what he enjoys, in rejoicing to see his will accomplished through the wide range of his dominions, and in being ourselves made instruments in accomplishing it.

The only character which is capable of enjoying these privileges, or indeed of considering them in the light of privileges, must be one which is in some measure conformed to God's character. This then is spiritual health, which evidently can only be derived from, or maintained by a love, a predominant love to God in his true character. But as man, from the constitution of his nature, was liable to choose differently from God's choice, and thus to fall into spiritual disease, it pleased the Divine wisdom to point out, in the form of an express law, the only source of spiritual health, saying, "Thou shalt love the Lord thy God with all thine heart;" and to sanction it by the penalty of exclusion in case of disobedience, and the promise of Divine privileges in case of obedience. Thus we see here also, obedience, spiritual health, and heavenly immunities, united by nature, as well as by positive law, on the one side; and disobedience, spiritual disease, and forfeiture, on the other.

Man disobeyed the commandment, he loved other things better than God; and thus subjected himself to the legal penalty, and at the same time was affected with that spiritual disease which disqualified him for being a member of God's family, even supposing that there had been no legal exclusion whatever.

When the mercy of God purposed to deliver man from this state of misery into which he had precipitated himself, it became his object to bring him back to spiritual health, and thus to make him partake of heavenly happiness. But the source of health still continued the same; an intelligent being could only become like God, by loving God in his true character. It became necessary then, that some manifestation of the Divine holiness and justice should be made, so interwoven with motives to gratitude, that he who believed the history of it should be constrained to love, not only the mercy of God, but even that awful and pure sanctity which cannot look upon iniquity.

We naturally esteem, and even love perfect justice, except in those cases where its condemning sentence falls upon ourselves. At the same time, if justice is compromised, even in our own favour, our gratitude is necessarily mingled with a degree of contempt or disesteem; so that it is the union of kindness and justice, in their highest degrees, which alone can attract perfect reverential love.

Now, supposing that such a manifestation of the character of God had been made, as that his mercy had seemed to overlook sanctity, and throw it into the shade, by affixing no stigma to transgression, our love could not have been accompanied by perfect reverence, and moreover, what is principally to be attended to, this love could not have the effect of healing our spiritual disease, because, not being attracted by the full and true character of God, it could not produce in us a resemblance to that true character which is the main object to be accomplished. This supposition is, of course, merely made for the sake of the argument, for it is absurd to suppose that God should manifest himself otherwise than in his true character.

A manifestation of unmixed justice in the Divine character must have been still more inefficacious. It could have attracted no love, and, of course, no resemblance; it could only have confirmed the sentence of condemnation, and thus have strengthened our enmity and despair, even whilst it might have compelled our respect.

In order to produce real spiritual health, the Divine manifestation must be such as to excite within our hearts a perfect complacency in all and each of the perfections of God; it must lead us to adopt his loves and hatreds, so to speak; it must exhibit sin to us, not only as fearful from its consequences, but as hateful in itself, and revolting to every feeling of affection and gratitude.

This manifestation of himself hath God made in the gospel of his Son. In that gospel he makes the fullest and freest offers of pardon and favour, but it is through the blood of atonement. God became man, and dwelt amongst us; he took upon himself our nature and the judicial sentence under which we lay on account of transgression. He showed the evil of sin, and the power of justice, by suffering the just for the unjust. The infinity of Godhead gave weight and dignity unspeakable to the sacrifice. He showed a love unmeasured, in that, when the authority of the Divine law required full satisfaction, he hesitated not to give himself a ransom for sinners. In this wondrous work, justice magnifies mercy, and mercy magnifies justice. The greatness of the sacrifice demonstrates the extent both of the Divine abhorrence for sin, and of the Divine love for sinners. When we sin against this Saviour, or forget him, we must feel that it is the basest ingratitude, it is trampling on that blood that was shed for us. The gospel further assures us, that this same God is ever present, with these same feelings toward us, with these same feelings toward sin—that he orders every event, and appoints every duty—that he offers us his listening ear, and his enabling Spirit, in all difficulties—and that he points us to a rest beyond the grave, where our resemblance to him shall be completed, and his joy shall be ours.

In this manifestation of the Divine character, the attributes of justice and mercy form a combination so amiable and so resplendent, that whilst our affections and esteem are chained to it, our very conception faints under it. We can here love perfect justice, because we are not under its condemnation; we can here adore perfect mercy, because it is unmixed with weakness or partiality. Sin, even in the abstract, is associated in our minds with sentiments of abhorrence as well as fear; and holiness with sentiments of affection as well as hope.

A growing resemblance to the character thus gloriously manifested is the necessary consequence of our love for it. This is a law of our nature. The leading objects of our thoughts and affections constitute the moulds, as it were, into which our minds are cast, and from which they derive their form and character. This fact ought to make us most watchful over the motions of our hearts; for it is only by a constant contemplation of the true character of

God, and by cherishing and exercising those affections and desires which arise out of this contemplation, that the Divine image is renewed in our souls. We are not to expect any mechanical or extraneous impression separate from that which the truth makes; for it is by the truth alone, known and believed, that the Holy Spirit operates in accomplishing that sanctifying work, which is itself salvation. When the soul, therefore, leaving God, chooses created things for its chief objects, these things become the moulds which impart to it their own fleeting character, and imprint on it their own superscription of vanity and death.

When this connection between loving an object and resembling it is considered, we can have no difficulty in discerning why faith in the gospel history is required in order to salvation. We cannot love that which we do not believe, and we cannot resemble that which we do not love. Hence it is that faith becomes a matter of such vital consequence. It is the very foundation of the whole Christian character, the very root of the tree.

If salvation had consisted simply in the removal of the judicial penalty denounced against sin—if this had been the sole scope of the work of Christ, it would have been unnecessary to have revealed the gospel history to men, or to have required their belief of it; because the atonement being made, their belief could neither add to it nor take from it. But when salvation is considered to express the renewed health of the soul, and when heaven and hell are considered as the names of opposite characters, necessarily connected, by the very nature of things, with certain happy or miserable consequences, and thus, when the revealed law of God is considered as explaining and declaring the particulars of a *constitution* which was originally mixed up with the elements of our being, rather than as enacting a new one, then we see the importance of faith, because it is the only medium through which the perfections of the Divine character can possibly make any impression on our minds; and unless our minds be so impressed as to excite our love, we cannot become like God, or, in other words, our spiritual health cannot be restored, nor improved. We are not called upon to believe anything for the mere sake of believing it, any more than we are called on to take a medicine for the mere sake of taking it; we are called on to believe the truth, on account of the healing influence that it has upon the mind, as we are called on to take a medicine on account of its influence on our bodily health.

It follows from this, that what is called doctrinal instruction, when properly applied, is really the most practical. No one would be considered as a practical physician who merely recommended his patients to be in good health, and painted the advantages of a good appetite, of bodily ease and vigour, whilst at the same time he did not apply the remedies which might lead to these effects. So likewise, he is not a practical teacher of religion who contents himself with exhorting his hearers to be in spiritual health, and to exhibit in their lives and conversations those Christian virtues which are the symptoms of spiritual health, whilst he does not anxiously and constantly, at the same time, inculcate upon them that view of the Divine character in Jesus Christ, which contains in itself means of powerful operation to renew and purify the mind, and which God himself has revealed as the appointed medicine for healing the diseases of the soul, and restoring it to health and vigour. It is possible that a physician either of souls or of bodies may be so engrossed with the beauty of his theory, that he may forget that application of it from which it derives its sole importance; but this error is not greater than the error of those who should dream of restoring health without the application of any means, or by such as are contrary to the obvious principles of the science which they profess.

Besides, although we can form a very accurate notion of what bodily health is, it is impossible for us to do this with regard to spiritual health, without comprehending, according to the measure of our capacities, the state and character of that eternal mind, who is the pattern, as he is the source, of all spiritual perfection. And this view cannot be taken without entering into and understanding the dealings of God with men, in the mission of Jesus Christ, which is represented in the Bible as by far the most striking and important manifestation of the Divine character with which the world has been favoured. So that it is a delusion to call upon men, or direct them to acquire spiritual health, unless at the same time the nature of this health is shown to them, by delineating the purposes of the life and death of Him in whom alone we can find the brightness of the Father's glory, and the express image of his person.

Health, neither mental nor bodily, can be gained without the use of the appropriate means. The means of bodily health are to be discovered by human experiment and science; but the means of spiritual health are contained in the gospel. Thus the mercy of God in Christ, and his holy abhorrence of sin manifested in perfect concord with mercy, constitute the spiritual medicine; and the object and result of its application is salvation or healing.

But although this renewal of spiritual health in man be the great object of the gospel, yet in itself it affords no ground of confidence before God; that is, it is no foundation on which we can rest our hope for pardon or acceptance with him; both because it is imperfect in itself, and because, even if it were perfect, it could not atone for past transgression. The only confidence which it is calculated to give is analogous to that confidence which a man feels when he finds his bodily health improving by the use of a particular regimen: he is satisfied of the advantage of the system, and he perseveres in it with alacrity. The ground of our hope before God continues the same, and this ground is the sacrifice of Christ for the sins of the world. The mercy and the justice manifested in this fact are, and continue for ever to be, the only food which can confirm and increase that spiritual health which they first gave. The moment that the soul begins to feed on any other food than this, the moment that it takes anything else for its chief joy, or hope, or confidence;—that very moment the health of the soul declines, the disease of sin gathers strength, and disorders the whole frame of the soul, withdraws the affections and faculties from the pursuit of those things which are eternal, and points them to passing shadows; relaxes all the energies of the spiritual life; displaces true joy, and hope, and peace, and substitutes in their room a joy that inebriates, and a hope that dies, and a peace that blindfolds, whilst it conducts to ruin. He who withdraws from the sacrifice of Christ, and places confidence in the spiritual health to which he has already attained, is like the man who would refuse his necessary food, and dream of supporting his life out of that stock of life which he had already enjoyed.

"My beloved brethren," says the Apostle, "be ye stedfast, unmovable, always abounding in the work of the Lord, forasmuch as ye know that your labour in the Lord is not in vain." This work consists in living under an ever-present sense of what God hath done for sinners, in the sacrifice of Jesus Christ. Faith means the conviction of the reality of things which we do not see. Now, in order that this conviction be of any use to us, it must be present with us. A man cannot be said to be under a conviction, unless it is upon his mind. If a man is convinced that particular precautions are necessary for his health, he will take these precautions; but as soon as he forgets the necessity, his precautions vanish. Thus, forgetfulness comes often to the same thing as an opposite conviction. The belief of the morning, if it be confined to the morning, will do us no good through the day. He that *believes* is saved, not he who *has* believed. The sole object of Christian belief is to produce the Christian character, and unless this is done nothing is done. Good bodily health has a value in itself, independently of the good digestion and good nourishment which produced it; so also spiritual health has a value in itself, independently of the correct belief which produced it. In both cases the effects are the objects of ultimate importance, but then they cannot exist without their causes; and when the causes cease to operate, the effects must also cease. To resemble God is the great matter, but we cannot resemble him without loving him; and we cannot love him in his true character without believing in his true character.[1]

In the character and writings of the Rev. SAMUEL RUTHERFORD the preceding remarks are most powerfully illustrated. He constantly presents the "blood of sprinkling" as the only effectual balm for the wounded conscience;

---

[1] The preceding remarks were furnished by Mr. Erskine for the edition of Rutherford's *Letters* published in 1825 by Messrs. Chalmers and Collins of Glasgow, in their Series of Select Christian Authors; the remarks which follow were furnished by another hand.

but it is, that the conscience, thus pacified, might be purged "from dead works to serve the living God." He constantly rests on the sacrifice of Christ for removing the guilt and condemnation of sin; but it is that, being delivered from the spirit of bondage and fear, he might serve God "in newness of spirit." He constantly looks to the perfect righteousness of Christ as the sure ground of his acceptance with God; but he no less looks to the perfection of Christ, that, by the transforming influence of such a contemplation, he might "be changed into the same image." He constantly directs his view to the glory and blessedness of those heavenly mansions which Christ has gone to prepare for his people; but it is that, having this hope in him, he might be prepared for these blessed mansions "by purifying himself even as Christ is pure."

While few have cherished a more cordial and unshaken faith in the obedience and death of Christ as the sole foundation of their hope for pardon and acceptance with God, few have more fully manifested the genuine and unfailing fruits of such a faith in the holiness and purity of their lives. Few have equalled him in their steady adherence to truth in the midst of persecution and suffering—or in greater devotion to the will of God, in everything he considered his duty, with such a fearless disregard of consequences—or in cherishing with greater care and tenderness a conscience void of offence towards God and towards man—or in making the work of personal sanctification more the business of their lives—or in labouring more abundantly to teach others the way of salvation, and extend the interests of pure and undefiled religion. In his life, no less than in his writings, he afforded a noble vindication of the doctrines of grace being doctrines according to godliness. "Holiness to the Lord" was the inscription which he endeavoured to write on every affection of his heart and on every action of his life; and knowing this to be the indispensable preparation for heaven, in his precious, and spiritual, and edifying Letters, he constantly breathes no less after purity than peace. In obedience to the apostolic injunction, his great endeavour was to keep himself in the love of God, and it was by maintaining in his soul a rejoicing sense of this love, and of peace and reconciliation with God, that he was enabled to offer the hourly and ever-burning incense of a heart devoted in all its affections to Him, as the God of his redemption.

T. E.

www.ingramcontent.com/pod-product-compliance
Lightning Source LLC
Chambersburg PA
CBHW031901220426
43663CB00006B/721